W9-BGB-855

Releasing Kings for Ministry in the Marketplace

John S. Garfield
and
Harold R. Eberle

Worldcast Publishing
Yakima, Washington

First Printing, April, 2004

Worldcast Publishing
P.O. Box 10653
Yakima, WA 98909-1653 USA
509-248-5837
email: office@worldcastpublishing.com
Web Site: www.worldcastpublishing.com

ISBN 1-882523-26-1
Cover by Paul Jones

Printed in the United States of America

What Others Are Saying

Here is my endorsement for your great new book: If you have any doubt that what you do in the workplace is not just a job, but a true, God-assigned ministry, *Releasing Kings* will make you a believer. This book is a clear road map toward exciting new freedom for the saints in the Body of Christ.

— C. Peter Wagner, Presiding Apostle
International Coalition of Apostles

Releasing Kings For Ministry in the Marketplace is a refreshing look at what God wants to do through us in the workplace. The authors model bridge building as a business leader and minister write together. They offer biblical insights into the roles of prophets, priests, and kings. Your assumptions will be challenged, your faith enlarged, and your courage increased as you read these words. Creativity, mentoring, and transformation will be the results in the lives of those leaders who experience Jesus Christ in their workplace. This will be a helpful resource for both workplace leaders and pastors.

— Kent Humphreys, President
Fellowship of Companies for Christ

Courageous! *Releasing Kings* is a bold and exciting introduction to the new frontier of Marketplace ministry and evangelism. It is a must-read for business people and professionals who want to understand and empower their calling to proclaim the Good News to their community and the world.

— Patty and Roger Stewart
Book Quest, Centralia, WA

Insightful and anointed! The marketplace is the new frontier for ministry and evangelism. Until now it has been one of the most misunderstood mission fields we have faced. The concept of *Releasing Kings for Ministry in the Marketplace* is a call to empower a new generation of business leaders who exemplify Christian character and zeal for reaching the lost. It is also a challenge to seek new resources for support of ministry and evangelism and to explore innovative ministry opportunities at home, abroad, and through all strata of society. John and Harold have unlocked the door for men and women of vision and action to prosper and expand God's Kingdom.

— Stephan Brown
"The Network" Threshold Resourcing
Phoenix, AZ

Steve Brown gave me a draft of your new book. It is reshaping my life and setting me free, seriously. I am an engineer, a manufacturer and a former pastor; the King idea feels right.

— Andy Briesmeister
Selah, WA

You have delivered something rare and significant from the heart of God, through this book. You have come a long way since Bible Way and your Methodist days. It took a lot of life and experience to have the whiskers to see and say these things. As I read your book, I learned and saw things more clearly that I already believed. It is a timely book, in my opinion. It was for me. I believe thousands of believers are hungry for this, even though they may not know it. Believers need to be equipped with right thinking.

I appreciated your matter-of-fact candor in making radical statements. You came across with a clean, healthy attitude, not with reaction or sour grapes, even though much of what you teach could be inflammatory to those trapped in the status quo. Sometimes it takes a cowboy to call a spade a spade, huh!

I believe what you are doing is love in action. Love takes initiative to bring change. It is a lot of work for you to write a book and try to get it in the hands of the people. I pray God will abundantly prosper it and shoot each one as an arrow to the target. It is bold! Stretching! Radical! But on target, I feel. It's like a chiropractic adjustment. The average believer will feel the crunch somewhere.

This is the kind of message we need to see the earth covered with the glory of the Lord and real evangelism happen. Daily in my shop I talk to believers who are virtually ineffective in evangelism, even pastors and leaders. I would like copies of this book to give out. God bless you.

— Wayne Hayworth
Portland, OR

Throughout the World, something unprecedented is happening, supernaturally and beyond the norm. Believers and non-believers are coming together in the Marketplace as they come together in the art of business. This book brings to all who read it a spanning of the denominational and non-denominational believers, a recognition of specific interests in God in the pursuit of our daily lives. I've been touched and am changed by this eye-opening book.

-- Richard O. Tedeschi
President, Radiant Light Broadcasting TV
TriCities, WA

Releasing Kings for Ministry in the Marketplace by John Garfield and Harold Eberle is a must read for both church leaders and those called to the marketplace. This refreshing book will be used by the Lord to prepare the church of our generation for the coming harvest. I highly recommend it! May the Lord release His kings, His priests, and His prophets to honor one another and then labor together with Him to bring in the harvest.

— Larry Kreider
International Director,
DOVE Christian Fellowship International (DCFI)
Lititz, PA

Table of Contents

Part IV: The Personal Lives of Kings

Foreword
By John L. Sandford

For too long the church has been mired in the mud of negative theologies and eschatologies, unable to speak with effectiveness to the business community, who must, by nature, build with positive hopes—or their projects, which necessarily must be planned years in advance, never would begin. For countless years the Church has proclaimed it must move out from within its four walls into ministry in the marketplace. Currently many of the Lord's prophets are pronouncing with great emphasis and urgency that this is the time when our Lord is going to prosper those who will have the faith and courage to step forward into ministry in the marketplace. But the Church has not known how.

John Garfield and Harold Eberle have responded to the Lord's call. This book is a breath of fresh air to those suffocating under the old wine skins of ministry. John and Harold make clear that those called into ministry in the marketplace are "Kings" who are not to be confined to ministry within the four walls of the church as "Priests." John and Harold blow a clear trumpet to all business men and women to arise in their own giftings, within their own "secular' places of work, to know irrevocably that their allegedly secular work is the holy ground of their callings, their giftings, and their ministries. They blow away the halitosis of centuries of false breathing in rooms of tiny concepts inside stifling walls to celebrate the value and worth of all that men and women do to build God's

Kingdom "out there" on Earth. They demolish the binding concept that true Christians, of course, must leave the workaday world to answer God's call upon their lives in some kind of church vocation that could be called "holy"—and is not truly theirs as God's Kings in the world. Jesus was a carpenter from his youth until He was thirty. Paul was a tentmaker who ministered where he was in the workaday world.

God is a builder, preparing for better and greater ways and constructs right here on earth. He is making a new heaven—and a new earth. *Releasing Kings For Ministry in the Marketplace* aims to set free the vast army of the Lord's servants to be who they are, God's sons and daughters who partner with Him in building His kingdom in the world.

This book declares that we must set our people free to be as creative, energetic, and innovative as the Holy Spirit prompts, right where they are in the marketplace. We must lift away the false demands and guilt that these servants of the Lord are not being truly spiritual unless, or until, they throw off their own callings and accept truly "spiritual" tasks for which they are neither called nor gifted!

The Church needs desperately to hear this message. I say, "Buy not one copy, get a copy into the hands of every business man and woman in your church—and outside it." God, and this book, want to bring forth the "princes who will rule justly" of Isaiah 32:1. "And each will be like a refuge from the wind, and a shelter from the storm, like streams of water in a dry country, like the shade of a huge rock in a parched land" (vs 2).

— John L. Sandford
Founder, Elijah House

Preface

Finding purpose is the hallmark of motivation in vocational and spiritual life. Personal destiny is captivating, empowering, and releasing. We've used "Kings" to refer to this dynamic. There is an entrepreneurial, conquering, creative, and contagious aspect of Christianity that is sweeping over the Body of Christ. We've tried to capture the spirit of this present wind in words that span the thrill of what we are experiencing personally with what can be prophetically anticipated in the marketplace through a movement of Kings.

God has prepared a generation of Joshuas who are hungry for a tangible expression of their purpose (ministry) and receptive to the revelation of God's Spirit Who will escort them (theology). The result is fruitful people naturally liberated into their passion for work, their compassion for people, and their love for the Lord Jesus. They have permission to dream (faith) and they are innovative, self-starters who see their dreams realized (works).

The invitation to leave the pew and enter ministry in the marketplace will be stretching. Our attempts to distinguish those who minister in the marketplace from those employed by the local church may sound as if we're minimizing pastoral ministry. What we really believe is that Kings will strengthen the local church by expressing her evangelism. They will come with joy "bringing their sheaves with them." Though Kings minister outside the local church, they are still part of the Larger Body of Christ (Church) and a specific local body (church) led by a pastor.

We are using the term "marketplace" instead of "workplace" to describe the domain of kings because it is more entrepreneurial...even though we risk the "sales" label. This book is not about how to be successful at your job; it's about how to be successful at your dream. Allow the Lord to unveil the oneness of your vocation, your avocation, your ministry, and God's purpose for your life. You'll be amazed at the blessing that flows from a life integrated in those four areas. The ensuing passion is highly contagious. The real work of the ministry is in the marketplace; it's the saints who take up the mantle of "Kings" who will carry the great commission into all the world.

The idea of marketplace ministry has a few pioneers on whose shoulders we stand. Leaders such as Rich Marshall, Ed Silvoso, Bill Hamon, and Peter Wagner have done the Body of Christ a great service. They have led the way in recognizing the anointing and ministry of people who never preach from a pulpit; yet they still are called by God to expand the Kingdom outside the four walls of our local churches. We're grateful for the insight to connect the ministry and the mindset with a theological framework that will release the next phase of filling the Earth with His glory.

James Bryson helped us organize and edit the first drafts. Annette Bradley was our final editor. Numerous friends read the manuscript and added their suggestions and advice. We owe them all a great deal for making this book a reality.

Most of all, we thank the Lord of the Harvest for setting marketplace ministers free in this hour.

Introduction

God is preparing us for the next great revival which will begin and flourish throughout the marketplace. He is now positioning Christians strategically throughout all areas of society: business, government, education, entertainment, services, communication, transportation, agriculture, social services, and the arts. The Lord is opening doors of creativity, productivity, and prosperity that will make our vocations meaningful and delightfully fulfilling. Instead of a remnant just holding on for a rapture, we are busy—aggressively expanding God's Kingdom into the marketplace, which is the heart of our cities. Just as the New Testament believers before us, we are going to turn the world upside down (Acts 17:6).

This book is to inspire and propel Christians into this move of God—to find their places in marketplace ministry.

A New Breed of "Ministers"

When people first become Christians, they get excited about finding their gifts, entering their ministry callings, and operating in the power of God. It is the beginning of connecting to their destinies. There is nothing more exciting or rewarding than knowing that God is working through them to heal, encourage, or save someone for eternity.

Unfortunately, the path from salvation to ministry usually doesn't go smoothly. Though willing and excited to be used by God, most Christians are not called to full-time church staff positions, and the congregations could not support all of them, even if they were. In an effort to use their talents in local churches and develop ministry gifts, the idea of "lay ministry" was developed, allowing the laity to be involved in church ministry with the time they could spare from their secular vocations and family commitments. The intent was good, but several problems ensued. It made the church introverted (less evangelistic) and somewhat competitive. Only about 2% of Christians work on a church staff. The rest have to be part time in the ministry and full time in secular work. (If you have a secular job, you will recognize this as unpaid overtime.) It depletes the energy, drive, and zeal of sincere Christians willing to give themselves to ministry.

The answer lies in understanding the roles of "Kings" and "Priests" in the Body of Christ. In this book we will talk about Christians (men and women) working as Kings in the marketplace, taking dominion, walking as royalty, and establishing the Kingdom of God in the Earth. At the same time, there are men and women of God who serve in the Church as Priests, reconciling people to God and equipping them to walk in God's ways. Even though all Christians are Kings and Priests unto God, we each find our primary calling to either the marketplace or the Church. Great blessings come when we recognize these callings and allow people the freedom to serve where they are called and anointed by God.

Some who read these pages may conclude that we have gone too far in separating the kingly and priestly roles. Again, we acknowledge that all Christians are both Kings and Priests unto God. In separating these two roles our hearts are not to exclude anyone from their involvement in both the marketplace and the Church, but rather *to encourage Christians to excel in their primary calling*.

Kings possess the personality, calling, gifting, and ministry to reach the hearts of our cities and all of society. Priests, on the other hand, are gifted uniquely by God to function within the Church, attending to the duties of feeding, caring for, and equipping God's people. The two personality types, while compatible, are created by God for different functions; as such, each is most fruitful in his/her natural environment: Kings in the Kingdom; Priests in the Temple.

Pastors (under the category of Priests) tend to motivate their congregations to focus all of their ministry energies within the church. When Kings, who are competitive by nature, become committee leaders, deacons, board members, or elders, and start "helping" the pastor with decisions about running the church, they lose their effectiveness (and often their welcome). Kings may have pastoral hearts and prophetic anointings but their primary calling is not inside the church; it is out in the marketplace expanding the Kingdom of God.

Now is the time for Kings to be released and activated to take the power and message of the Gospel into the world.

Imagine

Imagine the growth of Christianity and the city-wide impact that would occur if 98% of the Body of Christ stepped into kingly anointings, leaving the pastoral care to those who truly are called to it. Kings would be in church on Sunday receiving a rich equipping from the Priests (pastors, teachers, and other anointed church leaders) to be deployed the remaining six days to minister at work. Imagine a small business owner who perceived of him/herself as a minister called of God to care for and lead his/her employees. Imagine God's favor to multiply financial blessings to an advertising executive through an anointing for creativity. Imagine gifts of the Spirit operating in the marketplace to reach the lost one minute and to make financial decisions the next. Imagine the wall between "secular" and "spiritual" crumbling. Imagine Kings in the marketplace ministering in the Spirit as freely as Priests minister in the Church. Think about being employed by God in a workplace vocation that causes you to seek Him the same way that a pastor seeks God in preparing the message for Sunday.

Purpose

To understand God's design of Kings and Priests, it is necessary to have the biblical foundation that explains and supports it. To that end, we are going to acquaint you with a contemporary version of Kings (the modern equivalent of Abraham, Joseph, Moses,

Joshua, Nehemiah, David, Solomon, Daniel...) and explore their godly motivations, the nature of their ministries, and their unique personality. We also are going to explore the biblical foundation for a King's ministry motivations, examining topics such as, "Who is God?" "Who are we?" and "What is our future?"

In the Bible, as in present day, Kings are the ones who get things done whenever God is moving, shaking, or expanding His Kingdom. It's an honor to have a calling to the marketplace—that is where the action is.

You, the reader, may sense such a calling on your life. The ramifications of having a kingly ministry in the marketplace will set your heart on fire. A compassionate Father has some new land with your name on it. You are being invited to talk to God and hear His voice. He is asking you to share your dreams, and then He is giving you the authority to implement them. You are going to find that your heart's desire matches God's heart more than you realized. When you see it, you will be surprised and delighted at the doors that open in every area of your life...you'll no longer be "just a servant."

> *"I no longer call you servants, because a servant does not know his master's business. Instead, I have called you friends, for everything that I learned from my Father I have made known to you...."* (John 15:15)

This book is dedicated to the 98% of us who sit in

the pews, admire the ministers in front, and wish God would use us in a dynamic way. Our prayer is that this book will be a tool of the Holy Spirit to release your heart for ministry into a realm that really does produce results—the workplace. Our lives will naturally bear the character, works, and fruit of Christ as we are rooted in a relationship with the Father, growing in the soil of sound doctrine and motivated by love to expand His Kingdom. The Lord is opening doors of creativity, productivity, prosperity, and ministry that make our vocations in the marketplace delightfully fulfilling.

An Overview

Part I defines the interaction between Kings and Priests. The groundwork is laid to understand the ministry, the Scriptural basis, and the potential for Kings to impact the mission of the Kingdom.

Part II examines the motivational foundation in our beliefs about the nature of God (Who is God?), the nature of humanity (Who am I?), and eschatology (Where are we going?). Our goal in presenting this theology is to anchor Kings in a doctrinal system which supports the risks and adventure of being one of God's Great Ones.

Part III explains the ministry of Kings and what makes them tick. We will see why Kings are bold, creative, competitive, etc. We will embrace a personal God who shares His business with Kings, and we'll understand a King's passion and drive.

Part IV shows how Christians who relate to God personally are delightfully more relational than those who relate only to a cold, impersonal God. Kings are mentors and leaders who connect with people instead of just directing them. They never lose their childlike ability to dream as they pursue their hearts' desires. They have a prayer life that consists of "asking and receiving." They love to mentor others and share the secrets of their successes. They have plans to impact generations by passing their financial and spiritual heritages on to others.

Let Us Encourage and Equip You

This book has two authors. John Garfield is bi-vocational, being a successful engineer and manager in a large corporation, while at the same time founding two churches. Harold R. Eberle is an author, minister, and popular motivational speaker who has founded several schools and orphanages in developing nations. Even though these two authors combined their thoughts and worked closely together, it is written in the first person singular from John's perspective. This is because John has taken the lead in writing most of this book (Parts I, III and IV) and most of the examples come from his life. From this point on when you read "I," realize that you are hearing the words of John, with Harold looking over his shoulder, shouting wholehearted agreement and wrestling for control of the keyboard.

Part I
Kings in the Marketplace, Priests in the Church

Jesus declared: "The Kingdom of God is at hand!" This declaration, "at hand," meant that the Kingdom was within reach and available for people to experience now, in this life. Our Lord explained that the Kingdom was within the hearts of people and within their midst (Luke 17:21). He also taught that the Kingdom was growing in the Earth as seeds cast into the soil (Matt. 13:24-30). Indeed, the Kingdom is here and it is growing.

Two thousand years ago, Jesus ascended into Heaven and sat down at the right hand of the Father. He now rules over the Kingdom of God. He was given authority over all of Heaven and Earth. He reigns and will continue to reign until a day when every knee bows and every tongue confesses that He is Lord (I Cor. 15:25-28).

Many have missed the present reality of this Kingdom. They think that the Kingdom of God is a place which Christians only can experience after they die and go to Heaven. But the Apostle Paul explained that the Kingdom of God is for now, and it consists of righteousness, peace, and joy in the Holy Spirit (Rom. 14:17). In another passage, Paul explained that the Kingdom of God consists of power (I Cor. 4:20). Of course, we will not experience the fullness of the Kingdom until we see Jesus, but we must understand that it is available for us today. The power, the joy, the righteousness and peace are for God's people now. All who put their faith in King Jesus are citizens of this great Kingdom (Col. 1:13).

But Jesus is not only Lord over a Kingdom, He also is building a Temple; that is, a House for God to indwell. Unlike the Temple in the Old Testament times, the Temple which Jesus is building is being made out of living stones—His people. Jesus told us that this Temple would be victorious and the gates of hell would not prevail against it (Matt. 16:18).

The Church is not the Kingdom. To see this distinction, think of the Temple and the Kingdom in Solomon's day. Solomon's Temple was glorious, yet small compared with the Kingdom which encompassed the Temple and reached to lands far beyond it. In similar fashion, the Church is glorious, yet smaller than the Kingdom of God over which Jesus reigns.

Another distinction between the Church and the Kingdom is seen in the purposes for which they exist. The primary purpose of the Church is to be a dwelling place for God. Of course, there are other purposes, such as equipping the saints and sending people out for ministry, but the foremost purpose is to be a community of believers in whom God dwells. In contrast, the primary purpose of the Kingdom is to establish the rulership of Jesus Christ. Hence we pray:

> *Your kingdom come.*
> *Your will be done,*
> *On earth as it is in heaven.* (Matt. 6:10)

We pray for His Kingdom to be manifested here on Earth. We want to see the will of our Lord Jesus fulfilled even outside the walls of our churches, in business, government, education, entertainment, services, communication, transportation, agriculture, social services, the arts, and all areas of society.

The Church and the Kingdom are Distinct

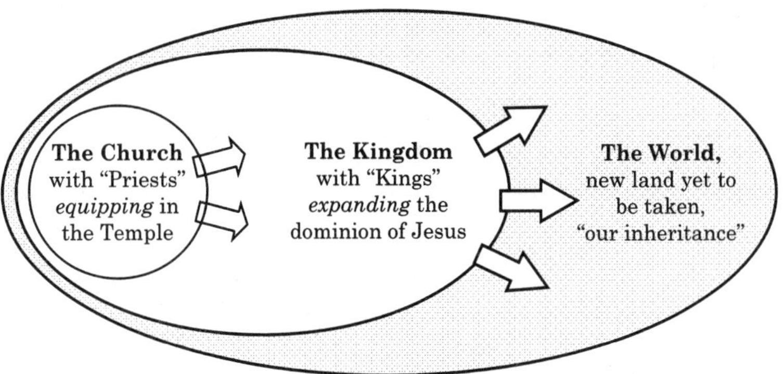

The Church is not the Kingdom, but she has the keys of the Kingdom (Matt. 16:19). Keys lock and unlock doors. Indeed, as a leader in the Church I can use those keys right now either to open or lock closed the doors of the Kingdom. If I discourage you, tell you that you are ineffective, and that God does not want you to be a success, then I am using the authority I have as a leader to cause you to be less effective in the world. If I tell you that the only place to serve God is within the four walls of the building, I will lock the doors of the Kingdom so it will be difficult for you to experience the power of God in the marketplace. If I tell you that the world is so big and evil that we cannot change it, then I will undermine your faith and hinder you from walking in God's blessings.

On the other hand, if I boldly declare to you that Jesus reigns and He wants to rule through your life, then I empower you. If I tell you the truth that Jesus will be with you wherever you go—into business, politics, art, or education—then more likely you will step out in confidence. If I speak of the goodness of God and reassure you that God wants to give you wisdom and prosper you, then I will release the creativity and blessings of God into your life. If I use the keys by speaking the promises and words of God, then you may discover a God who is at work in you and on your behalf.

It is time for you to be released into the Kingdom. It is time to discover who you are.

What does it mean to be a King and Priest? In the Old Testament times a person had to born of the kingly family in order to become a king. They had to be born into the priestly family line to become a Priest. But Jesus Christ came into the Earth as both King and Priest. Now He sits at the right hand of the throne of God as King, and He is making intercession for us as the Highest Priest. He rules over a Kingdom and He is building a Temple.

Here is the good news. When you became a Christian you were born into God's family. You are now of the kingly and priestly family line. Yes, you are a King and a Priest. Your primary calling may be to serve within the Temple (Church), or it may be to expand the Kingdom on Earth. Either way, you will serve Him with your whole heart, and He will be with you, even to the ends of the Earth.

This understanding opens the door for marketplace ministry and the role of Kings endeavoring to expand the Kingdom.

Eureka! We see that Priests (pastors, teachers, and other anointed church leaders) have a role in the Church. Kings (Christians in the marketplace) have a role out in the world, expanding the Kingdom of God. Our attempts to close the clergy/laity gap fall short because God isn't trying to make Priests out of everyone or to keep the congregation busy (and introverted) inside the local church. Most of us have ministries outside our church—expanding the Kingdom. We are the Abrahams and Isaacs (businessmen), Joshuas and Calebs (military personnel), Josephs and Davids (government officials), and Nathans and Daniels (Prophets in government) of this present age. We can expand the Kingdom of God into every area of society.

The Apostle Paul asked the question, "How will they go unless they are sent?" (Rom. 10:15). The implied answer is that they will not go. So I am writing to send you, to tell you that it is okay to expand the Kingdom of God into your corner of the world. Be a King!

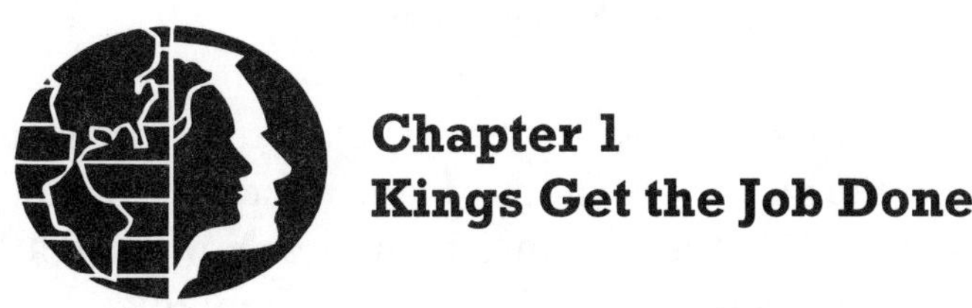

Chapter 1
Kings Get the Job Done

In 458 BC a Jewish Priest named Ezra returned to Jerusalem to rebuild the city. It had been destroyed over 100 years earlier by the Babylonians who took the Jews into captivity. Ezra's work stagnated before he could manage to rebuild the walls and the gates of the city.

A full 13 years later Nehemiah arrived at Jerusalem, took charge of the project, and had the walls up in 52 days.

> *So the wall was completed on the twenty-fifth of Elul, in fifty-two days.* (Neh. 6:15)

That was an historic accomplishment.

As a Priest, Ezra was well-versed in the law of Moses (Ezra 7:5). Nehemiah, on the other hand, was a government official—the King's cupbearer (Neh. 1:11), who later was appointed to be the governor of Jerusalem (Neh. 5:14). Both were anointed, godly men who served together.

> *...in the days of Nehemiah the governor and of Ezra the Priest....* (Neh. 12:26)

What Ezra could not accomplish by himself as a Priest was achieved easily by Nehemiah in a "kingly" capacity.

Think about the great names that you know from the Bible. Perhaps Abraham, Isaac, Jacob, Joseph, Moses, Joshua, or David come to mind. Now, list all the Priests you can remember. Draw a blank? You may think of one or two Prophets, but leaders identified strictly as Priests do not stand out. Why is this? The reason is that God always has used Kings as the movers and shakers in the Kingdom.

Priests (pastors, teachers, and other church leaders) play an important role in the Temple (Church), but it's a role that has a maintenance implication. They keep families healthy by feeding them the Word. They counsel, encourage, heal, marry, and bury. They shepherd, feed, and equip God's people. Pastors naturally gravitate to a peaceful, healthy atmosphere and have a godly motivation to keep their congregations happy and maturing.

In contrast, Kings go to war. They establish their authority. They move people into new territories—stretching people out of their comfort zones to expand the Kingdom of God on this Earth.

Historically, Kings have been leaders who worked closely with Priests and Prophets. They were talented people with the resources to get things done. They also were well-versed in God's Word and occasionally could operate in prophetic ministries themselves.

In the Old Testament, we see that Daniel spent his life in a governmental (kingly) role but used a prophetic gift to interpret dreams. Abraham was a businessman who raised livestock and became the most powerful man in his day. Moses was a national leader. Joshua was a military leader. They all had a calling as Kings to possess the inheritance God gave His people.

In the New Testament, we see the Lord pressing major initiatives with Kings again. Neither Jesus nor any of the 12 disciples came from priestly lines. The major players were Kings in the ministry sense. They had influence and power in the marketplace; some even had significant wealth.

Notice that the Kings did more than provide for the Temple of God. This is important because some church leaders today want to release the Kings, but they think the King is to use all of his profit to provide for the Priests and the Temple. Of course, the Kings will be blessed financially, and they will be generous in providing for God's house, but they are called to do more than that. Kings have the calling of God to extend the rulership of Jesus Christ into all of the world. They expand the Kingdom to fill the Earth with His glory.

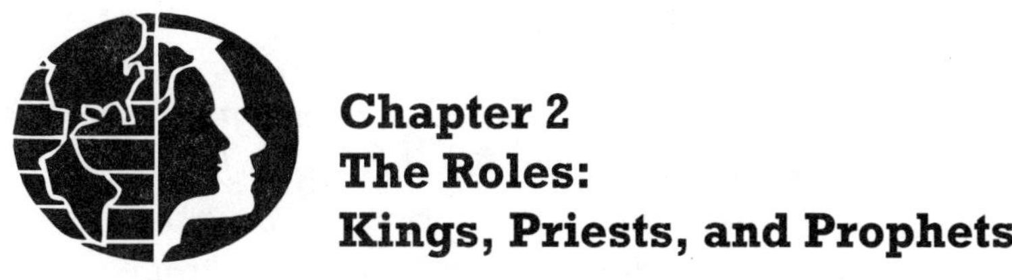

Chapter 2
The Roles:
Kings, Priests, and Prophets

In the Old Testament times, God raised leaders as Kings and Priests. Of course, we cannot totally equate today's Kings and Priests to those of Bible days, but we can understand differences in their roles by examining God's plan for their lives.

In addition to Kings and Priests, we also will take a quick look at the role of Prophets, for these people of God often work alongside the Kings and Priests.

Kings

> *When you enter the land the LORD your God is giving you and have taken possession of it and settled in it, and you say, "Let us set a King over us like all the nations around us," be sure to appoint over you the King the LORD your God chooses. He must be from among your own brothers. Do not place a foreigner over you, one who is not a brother Israelite. The King, moreover, must not acquire great numbers of horses for himself or make the people return to Egypt to get more of them, for the LORD has told you, "You are not to go back that way again." He must not take many wives, or his heart will be led astray. He*

> *must not accumulate large amounts of silver and gold. When he takes the throne of his kingdom, he is to write for himself on a scroll a copy of this law, taken from that of the Priests, who are Levites. It is to be with him, and he is to read it all the days of his life so that he may learn to revere the LORD his God and follow carefully all the words of this law and these decrees and not consider himself better than his brothers and turn from the law to the right or to the left. Then he and his descendants will reign a long time over his kingdom in Israel.*
>
> (Deut. 17:14-20)

A few observations concerning Kings:

1. Notice that the Lord chose the Kings (vs. 15). The kingly anointing and ordination was just as sacred as the ordination of Priests in the Old Testament. It is the same today.
2. Kings are cautioned against materialism and other indulgences (vs. 16-17). Why? Kings have an anointing to accumulate resources and get things done. Their weaknesses, however, can be pride and independence.
3. Kings are cautioned to stay close to Scripture; to write it, keep it with them, and read it all the days of their lives (vs. 18-19).
4. Kings command the people. They have influence and exercise leadership.

Priests

The Priests, who are Levites—indeed the whole tribe of Levi—are to have no allotment or inheritance with Israel. They shall live on the offerings made to the LORD by fire, for that is their inheritance. They shall have no inheritance among their brothers; the LORD is their inheritance, as he promised them. This is the share due the Priests from the people who sacrifice a bull or a sheep: the shoulder, the jowls and the inner parts. You are to give them the firstfruits of your grain, new wine and oil, and the first wool from the shearing of your sheep, for the LORD your God has chosen them and their descendants out of all your tribes to stand and minister in the LORD's name always. If a Levite moves from one of your towns anywhere in Israel where he is living, and comes in all earnestness to the place the LORD will choose, he may minister in the name of the LORD his God like all his fellow Levites who serve there in the presence of the LORD. He is to share equally in their benefits, even though he has received money from the sale of family possessions. (Deut. 18:1-8)

The LORD said to Aaron, "You will have

> *no inheritance in their land, nor will you have any share among them; I am your share and your inheritance among the Israelites. I give to the Levites all the tithes in Israel as their inheritance in return for the work they do while serving at the Tent of Meeting."* (Num. 18:20-21)

A few observations concerning Priests:

1. They have no allotment nor inheritance. The Lord is their inheritance.
2. Priestly income comes from offerings and tithes (Deut. 18:1-4).
3. While Kings have great wealth, Priests do not.
4. The Priests' primary function is to minister to the Lord.

Here are a few more practical observations about Priests and the personalities that go with their roles:

1. Priests have a focus for God's people and they should not be weighed down by projects or material concerns. This principle is illustrated by the Apostles in Acts 6.2:

   > *So the Twelve gathered all the disciples together and said, "It would not be right for us to neglect the ministry of the word of God in order to wait on tables."*

2. Priests are the shepherds who leave the 99 sheep to retrieve the lost one. They hesitate to go faster than the slowest lamb. By contrast,

Kings rarely go slower than the fastest horse.

3. Priests have hearts for worship, since their greatest possession is the Lord Himself.
4. Priests are chosen by God. They are consecrated and ordained to be ministers to Him and His people.

Prophets

Now let's look at a key passage of Scripture to identify God's plan for Prophets.

> *The LORD said to me: "What they say is good. I will raise up for them a Prophet like you from among their brothers; I will put my words in his mouth, and he will tell them everything I command him. If anyone does not listen to my words that the Prophet speaks in my name, I myself will call him to account. But a Prophet who presumes to speak in my name anything I have not commanded him to say, or a Prophet who speaks in the name of other gods, must be put to death." You may say to yourselves, "How can we know when a message has not been spoken by the LORD?" If what a Prophet proclaims in the name of the LORD does not take place or come true, that is a message the LORD has not spoken. That Prophet has spoken presumptuously. Do not be afraid of him.* (Deut. 18:18-22)

A few observations concerning Prophets.

1. Prophets are introduced as those who guard against "detestable" practices (Deut. 18:12) of sorcery or divination.
2. Prophets can discern wrong motives and hidden behavior as if by a sixth sense.
3. Prophets speak God's voice. They often intercede in prayer, going before God for the people.
4. Prophets can fall into the excess of presumption when they go beyond the words, the method, or the timing of God (vs. 20). God holds them to severe accountability for this.
5. God endorses these prophetic ministries and holds people accountable to heed a Prophet's words (vs. 19).
6. Prophets sometimes are supported in unusual ways. For example, Elijah was fed by ravens (Kings 17:6), then by a widow with no food (Kings 17:14). Whereas Kings have businesses and Priests have the tithe, Prophets often were supported supernaturally. Today's Prophets often have itinerant ministries, and they are supported by special offerings or by "Kings" who provide direct support.

In the Scriptures we see Prophets working alongside Kings and Priests. God often used the Prophets to give direction, correct error, or help leaders make breakthroughs necessary for success. They can bless or curse. They can recognize anointings or attacks of the enemy. Prophets add a supernatural boost for the expansion for the Kingdom.

Chapter 3
The King's Personality: Bold, Competitive, and Creative

Kings rule. Kings conquer. Kings establish order.

The kingly mindset is greatly different from the stereotype we often carry of "spiritual people." Instead of quiet, humble, prayerful monks, Kings are typically colorful, bold, creative, and decisive. Kings are competitive about making progress and wealth. They naturally assert themselves to press for God's initiatives. Where Prophets proclaim God's direction, Kings take the unction, marshal the willing, and have great works accomplished before you can blink. The whole process can seem quite unholy to Priests.

Modern-day Kings come in several varieties. Although Kings today often focus on business and finance, there are also Kings in the arts, politics, communication, entertainment, and education who carry great influence. But in this chapter (and throughout most of this book), our focus is primarily on business-oriented Kings because they are the most visible in our communities.

Let's take a closer look at what makes a King tick.

1. **A Business Mindset** – What image comes to your mind when you think of King David as a young boy?

Growing up in a Methodist Church, I had a picture of David cradling a lamb in his arms. Most of us think of young David as a humble shepherd boy. That's the priestly interpretation of who he was.

Here's the King's version: David ran a sheep-ranching operation for his father to make a profit from wool and mutton. The sheep were bred to be hearty and tasty. David ran it well and the business was profitable. This was training ground so God could promote David to be a ruler.

2. The Competitive Spirit – Kings are aggressive. David killed lions and bears with a club! And he killed a giant with a rock and sling.

3. Motivated by Profit – When David visited his brothers on the front line and heard Goliath's taunts, here was his first question:

> *David asked the men standing near him, "What will be done for the man who kills this Philistine and removes this disgrace from Israel?"* (I Sam. 17:26)

David asked about the reward. He wanted to know what the profit motive was for this risky venture. When he found out that the reward was the King's daughter, Goliath's days were numbered.

4. Creativity and Craftsmanship – Bezalel is a classic example of a kingly ministry that had a work ethic and a talent. The Lord filled him with His Spirit and the result was skill and knowledge in all kinds of crafts. Bezalel and his followers built all the articles in the Temple—with an anointing. Normally, we would call this "secular" employment and it wouldn't count as inspired by God. But see what God called it:

> *Then the LORD said to Moses, "See, I have chosen Bezalel son of Uri, the son of Hur, of the tribe of Judah, and I have filled him with the Spirit of God, with skill, ability, and knowledge in all kinds of crafts—to make artistic designs for work in gold, silver, and bronze, to cut and set stones, to work in wood, and to engage in all kinds of craftsmanship.... Also I have given skill to all the craftsmen to make everything I have commanded you....* (Ex. 31:1-6)

In our home church, Scott is a welder. He often has to travel and work twelve-hour days. As a pastor, it's frustrating to see him come and go—it's difficult for him to carry responsibility in the church because of his travel. However, wherever he goes, his foreman sees his talent and gives him the most difficult welding jobs. Even though he works in a union, employers ask for him by name. Why? He has an anointing for his craft and he's very good at it.

Whenever he comes back, he usually brings a testimony about how he ministered to or led someone to the Lord on his last job. He doesn't just weld; he takes Jesus into the marketplace. They don't have chaplains on construction sites, and the workers are a crowd not normally in church on Sunday.

5. Covenant Wealth – The Bible has many promises for financial prosperity. God gives Kings the ability to produce wealth. It's a specific anointing that can express itself in ministry. These promises need to be undertaken in faith by Kings. We also should note that these promises are directed more at Kings than at Priests and Prophets, because Kings are the ones with the mandate to handle wealth.

> *You may say to yourself, "My power and the strength of my hands have produced this wealth for me." But remember the LORD your God, for it is he who gives you the ability to produce wealth, and so confirms his covenant, which he swore to your forefathers, as it is today.*
>
> (Deut. 8:16-18)

Church ministries can be supported by tithing and an occasional special offering. However, the mission of reaching cities and nations never will be supported by tithes alone. It requires the resources that only Kings can harness—for both theological and practical reasons.

6. Wisdom and Reputation – When the church in Acts ran into administrative problems, they chose men full of the Holy Spirit and wisdom, with a good reputation in the community. These men were not less spiritual than the apostles, they just had a different gift mix—they were Kings. They did more than just take care of practical matters, however.

Stephen and Philip went on to carry the mission of expanding the Kingdom.

> *"...Therefore, brethren, seek out from among you seven men of good reputation, full of the Holy Spirit and wisdom, whom we may appoint over this business; but we will give ourselves continually to prayer and to the ministry of the word." And the saying pleased the whole multitude. And they chose Stephen, a man full of faith and the Holy Spirit, and Philip, Prochorus, Nicanor, Timon, Parmenas, and Nicolas, a proselyte from Antioch, whom they set before the apostles; and when they had prayed, they laid hands on them. Then the word of God spread, and the number of the disciples multiplied greatly in Jerusalem, and a great many of the Priests were obedient to the faith.*
>
> (Acts 6:3-7 NKJV)

In this passage, the apostles (Priests) turned business over to Kings and gave themselves to their true calling—prayer and the ministry of the Word, and the equipping the saints for ministry. The seven appointed Kings were some of their best fruit. The result was:

1. The Word of God spread
2. Disciples multiplied in Jerusalem
3. Many Jewish Priests got saved

Just as Nehemiah built the wall in 52 days, when Kings got involved in this "business," we never hear of the problem again.

8. **Reaching Cities** – The parable of the ten minas makes the point that people who are faithful in small matters (such as money) are given more responsibility (such as cities).

> *"The first one came and said, 'Sir, your mina has earned ten more.' 'Well done, my good servant!' his master replied. 'Because you have been trustworthy in a very small matter, take charge of ten cities.' " "The second came and said, 'Sir, your mina has earned five more.' His master answered, 'You take charge of five cities.' "* (Luke 19:16-19)

Instead of seeing the responsibility for cities being given in Heaven, we need to see that city responsibility is part of our strategy for revival now! Kings with an anointing to multiply finances are the ones with the resources and mandate from God to impact our cities for Christ. This undertaking will be far more complicated and costly than any pastor or group of pastors could hope to undertake alone. Revival in our cities never will be funded with tithes that belong to our pastors (Priests). It will take the resources of Kings.

Chapter 4
Kings, Priests, and Prophets Working Together

Nearly all of God's major initiatives in Scripture had the three ministries of Kings, Priests, and Prophets working together. When David was King, the Prophet Nathan blessed David's initiative to prepare for building the Temple. Nathan also pointed out David's sin with Bathsheba. Throughout the Old Testament times, Kings sought the advice of Prophets before engaging in warfare. Priests offered the sacrifices that went with those initiatives.

Certain functions were required to be kept separate. Kings were not allowed to perform priestly functions. An impatient King Saul was sentenced to death for operating as a Priest when he offered sacrifices in place of Samuel, who was late in arriving (I Sam. 13:11). On the other hand, Saul previously practiced among the Prophets with no negative consequences (I Sam. 10:9-12).

Highlighting some of the difficulties these three groups have working together may help to understand their differences.

1. View of Wealth — By a King's standard, Priests are typically far less focused on wealth and possessions. Pastors, especially TV ministers, who are over-zealous for wealth seem out of place. On the other hand, some Priests spiritualize poverty and encourage others to adopt their simple lifestyles.

They say, "Blessed are the poor," and they believe humility and meekness are clothed in "holy" poverty. However, Kings simply can't absorb this message. Their ministries in the marketplace are rooted in their influence and prosperity.

Without promoting the excesses of materialism, we must make room in our theology for Kings to be channels for the finances, influence, power, and leadership to expand the Kingdom.

2. Leadership in Churches — The role of Prophets is to speak the voice of God. Priests have the responsibility to run the local church. When the church undertakes large-scale programs, projects, or fund-raisers, they often attract kingly ministries which can be tempted to run the whole church. Priests never can surrender the leadership of the church to a King without violating a spiritual principle. Kings don't serve God in the Temple; they serve Him in the marketplace.

3. City Transformation — We all want to see our cities won for Jesus, but at least here in the United States we have not seen it. Pastors have tried. They have unified, strategized, prayed, held city-wide meetings, and proclaimed themselves as the gatekeepers of their cities. What has been missing, however, is Kings. Pastors have stepped outside the Temple and haven't seen the benefit of working with Kings in the capacity for which God created them. Without the decisiveness of Kings, progress at these pastors' meetings is painfully slow. Decisions require committee unity before anything can move forward. Whatever timely thing God might want to do (prophetically) is compromised in scope, schedule, and cost to make sure no one is offended and to be sure it fits within the church budget. The result—very little is done. No surprise when you think about it. The very concept of taking a city is a kingly function that can be *blessed* by pastors/Priests, but not performed by them.

4. Decision Making — Our present theology places pastors of local churches as the highest authority and requires all activities to come under their "covering." A senior minister needs to be the highest authority in his/her church, and a Priest shouldn't be deterred from his/her vision for the church by Kings who really are called to expand the Kingdom outside the church.

By the same token, when Kings function in the marketplace, expanding the Kingdom, they are not simply an extension of the pastoral ministry in that city. Think about it. Historically, although Kings received guidance from Prophets and Priests, they made decisions on their own. Did David need anyone's permission to fight a battle? No. He heard from God and he took action. It was that simple.

Kings need to give themselves permission to hear God and act. They don't need their pastor's permission to operate outside the church. Of course, their actions should harmonize with the Priests', but Kings certainly won't get direction to function outside the church from most pastors. Kings are competitive, bold, creative, and decisive. For the most part, they will not learn to exercise those skills from a shepherding mentality.

Please hear this simple pattern for decision making. Pastors should make the decisions affecting the local church; they are God's Priests in the Temple. Kings should focus their initiatives toward the great commission—reaching outside the church and expanding the Kingdom. Kings should return from the marketplace with fruit—fruit that grows the local church. Pastors function primarily in the church; Kings function primarily in the marketplace.

We do want to note that even though the ministry of Kings is focused on the marketplace, we still see them attending and supporting their local church....worshipping beside prophets and apostles.

5. Apostolic Influence — Lastly, it's worth noting that the Church is on the eve of a great apostolic awakening. Just as the prophetic ministry came to the forefront in the 1980's, apostles similar to Paul, Peter, and James are beginning to appear with strengths in fathering, networking, church-planting, and miraculous signs and wonders.

When these priestly ministries begin to function, they will help release the kingly anointing and bridge the functions between pastors, Prophets and Kings. There will be greater initiative and authority for bold new moves outside the church that expand the Kingdom...and grow the Church as a by-product.

For future success we must understand the distinctions between Kings, Priests, and Prophets. All of God's major initiatives in the Bible were the result of these three ministries working together. When modern-day Kings begin to function, we'll see new land taken for the Kingdom. Kings will begin to inherit the whole Earth, as they possess what the Lord has for them. Pastors will see the impact of Kings in Church growth and evangelism. It's time to make room in our theology for this three-fold cord.

Chapter 5 Kings in the New Testament

Let's revisit some familiar verses and interpret them through the understanding we now have concerning Kings and Priests. Once we catch the vision for Kings, rereading the Bible will challenge many of our preconceived ideas.

Revisit the Rich Young Ruler

> *A certain ruler asked him, "Good teacher, what must I do to inherit eternal life?" "Why do you call me good?" Jesus answered. "No one is good—except God alone. You know the commandments: 'Do not commit adultery, do not murder, do not steal, do not give false testimony, honor your father and mother.'" "All these I have kept since I was a boy," he said. When Jesus heard this, he said to him, "You still lack one thing. Sell everything you have and give to the poor, and you will have treasure in heaven. Then come, follow me." When he heard this, he became very sad, because he was a man of great wealth. Jesus looked at him and said, "How hard it is for the rich to enter the kingdom of God! Indeed, it is easier for a camel to go through the*

> *eye of a needle than for a rich man to enter the kingdom of God."*
>
> (Luke 18:18-25)

This passage is directed to a "rich young ruler." These are the ingredients of someone with a kingly calling. The priestly interpretation of this passage is that the rich should realize they can't get into Heaven any easier than a camel can get through the eye of a needle (which was a narrow city gate). Therefore, they should sell everything they have, give to the poor, and be assured of eternal blessings.

I want to suggest another interpretation for this passage—as seen through the eyes of a King.

God is not in the business of promising wealth and/or influence to Kings and then taking it away. The message of this passage isn't, "Get rid of all the wealth"; it is that Kings should not put their wealth or influence ahead of God (Jesus tested this point in verse 22). The message of the Bible isn't that the rich can't get into Heaven; it's that none of us can get into Heaven apart from our repentance and Jesus' atonement.

Many well-meaning Christians have squandered wealth in an attempt to become poor and please God. That is wealth that could have been used to expand the Kingdom. In effect, they gave up their ministry as Kings because they were taught that there was no such thing.

In God's economy, Priests live off the tithe rather than the marketplace. Full-time ministers occasionally communicate an attitude that others owe them a living, that they are above having a job, that living by faith is waiting for checks to show up in the mail instead of working. Portions of those attitudes are fine for a Priest or Prophet, but poison for a King—or anyone else who needs to get out and earn a living and support a family.

The kingly interpretation of this passage is: "sell your current inventory to care for the poor and start obeying God." To a King, obeying God is similar to: "Go back to your business and figure out a way to help the poor by getting them jobs or showing them how to start their own businesses."

Since only two percent of us can serve God in full-time church staff positions, the rest of us need to rise to the opportunity and be Kings. To date, the primary model of spirituality to which we've been exposed is the one behind the pulpit. We need to reverence and appreciate our pastors in their priestly roles; they are doing a great job. But we can't pattern our ministries after the priestly model if we're destined to be Kings.

Peter, the Businessman

> *As Jesus was walking beside the Sea of Galilee, he saw two brothers, Simon called Peter and his brother Andrew. They were casting a net into the lake, for they were fishermen. "Come, follow me," Jesus said, "and I will make you fishers of men." At once they left their nets and followed him.* (Matt. 4:18-20)

I've heard many messages quoting this passage as Peter's response to the call to full-time ministry. The phrase, "...they left their nets and followed him," is taken to mean that Peter left his job to go into the ministry. For Priests, that's about how it goes down. However, Kings don't leave their secular vocations to start their ministry. Those jobs and businesses are a sacred part of a King's destiny. That is where they are called. Let's look at the second passage about Peter's employment and ministry.

> *Afterward Jesus appeared again to his disciples, by the Sea of Tiberias. It happened this way: Simon Peter, Thomas (called Didymus), Nathanael from Cana in Galilee, the sons of Zebedee, and two other disciples were together. "I'm going out to fish," Simon Peter told them, and they said, "We'll go with you." So they went out and got into the boat, but that night they caught nothing....* (John 21:1-14)

In this passage, we see Peter going back to fishing. The priestly interpretation is that Peter forsook his full-time ministry and resumed his fishing business. Further implied is that Peter's efforts were fruitless (fish-less?) until Jesus arrived and restored Peter to his ministry.

The kingly interpretation of this passage starts with an understanding that the nets and boats of that era could not sit idle for three-and-a-half years and then go back to sea without a major overhaul. In this passage, the nets didn't break and the boats didn't sink when Peter went to sea. Hello! According to the priestly interpretation, the boats were supposed to be left on shore three-and-a-half years. However, Peter, an experienced fisherman, would not have gone fishing with a vessel and nets that had sat idle on the beach for those years.

It is obvious that Peter's business continued, with or without his direct involvement. A relative may have run it or Peter himself may have run it bi-vocationally (working as a fisherman and a disciple). But the business did not sit idle.

Jesus used boats from which to preach and travel multiple times during His ministry (see the verses below). Whose boats did He use? Probably Peter's or some other businessperson's. We know from Luke that it was Peter's in one instance.

> *One day as Jesus was standing by the Lake of Gennesaret, with the people crowding around him and listening to the word of God, he saw at the water's edge* ***two boats****, left there by the fishermen, who were washing their nets. He got into one of the boats, the* ***one belonging to Simon****, and asked him to put out a little from shore. Then he sat down and taught the people from the boat.* (Luke 5:1-3) [Emp. Added]

After Peter began his ministry with Jesus, we see

the following passages from Mathew.

> *Then he [Jesus] got into the boat and his disciples followed him.* (Matt. 8:23)
>
> *Jesus stepped into a boat, crossed over and came to his own town.* (Matt. 9:1)
>
> *Such large crowds gathered around him that he got into a boat and sat in it, while all the people stood on the shore.* (Matt. 13:2)
>
> *When Jesus heard what had happened, he withdrew by boat privately to a solitary place.* (Matt. 14:13)
>
> *Immediately Jesus made the disciples get into the boat and go on ahead of him to the other side, while he dismissed the crowd.* (Matt. 14:22)

While Scripture is not detailed on these points, it is clear that for boats to be readily available to Jesus, His disciples either had access to them or were well-connected with those who did. The fact that these boats were used frequently for extended periods of time is evidence that they were probably under the ownership of one of the disciples. Peter or his brother, Andrew, seem the likely choices. Regardless, the fact that Peter's equipment stayed in working order for the years he was with Jesus is evidence enough that his business stayed afloat, and he did not sever his connection with it.

Paul Had a Business

Paul is another example of someone who messes up our priestly concept of full-time ministry. We know he was an apostle. We know he received some of his financial support from donations. We also know he had a business (with employees) that supported both his own ministry and the ministry of his friends.

> *Paul went to see them, and because he was a tentmaker as they were, he stayed and worked with them. Every Sabbath he reasoned in the synagogue, trying to persuade Jews and Greeks.* (Acts 18:2-4)

> *You yourselves know that these hands of mine have supplied my own needs and the needs of my companions. In everything I did, I showed you that by this kind of hard work we must help the weak, remembering the words the Lord Jesus himself said: "It is more blessed to give than to receive."* (Acts 20:34-35)

> *Or is it only I and Barnabas who must work for a living?* (I Cor. 9:6)

We can take home a couple of lessons from these passages:

1. We need to appreciate Paul's heart for ministry and his willingness to work for it. We need to extend that appreciation to contemporary kingly ministries that provide their own support and let their cups run over to support others.

2. We shouldn't idolize full-time ministries. How many conferences are held with sessions or luncheons open only to full-time ministers? The unsaid message is that they are more valuable, more spiritual, and somewhat exclusive. If the Apostle Paul came to these conferences, he wouldn't be able to attend the sessions! This type of exclusive treatment sends the wrong message to the Pauls of our day. We need to value our Kings and realize that they are the means to achieve local evangelism and missions...just as Paul did.

Chapter 6
Imagine Discipling Nations

Christians focus on winning the lost and bringing revival to our cities and nations. But take a hard look at our plan to take the Gospel to the ends of the Earth. Does anyone know what our plan is? Some of the huge, well-known ministries have a plan, but the average pastor does not, nor is he/she capable of developing a plan to take his/her region for God. Of course, Christianity is growing across the world. Yet we know there is more growth and expansion needed than we currently are experiencing. In reality, very little happens within a few blocks of our homes.

Although my city has many healthy churches with great pastors, Washington State is one of the "least churched" states in the US. So, while it's not hard to find a good church in our town, our communities still have a large population of un-churched people. Sure, we want to see places such as Iraq and Africa blessed with the Gospel. But we want to see our own communities touched by God, as well. The idea that we're waiting for a sovereign move of God for revival isn't very satisfying. In my case (I'm 52), I've been waiting for that revival for 30 years. Today my heart yearns to see God's people mobilized to reach their communities and entire world.

Kings are a huge part of the answer. Imagine turning the city fathers loose, (they already have wealth and influence in our cities), with the concept of reaching their own population for Christ. If we, the Body of Christ, gave them permission, we'd be amazed at the result. Imagine Kings in the city's business, arts, government, and education, strategizing across denominational barriers to reach their communities for Christ.

It will happen. We already see it beginning.

Our community has a local medical outreach for those without insurance. It's staffed with volunteer Christian doctors, nurses, dentists, counselors, and accountants who have banned together to give their Saturdays to meeting this need. They share a common goal that reflects the heart of God, and they are working together to make it happen.

These are not earth-shaking initiatives but they are the beginning of Kings working outside the church to make an impact on our communities. It's exciting and there's an anointing on it that everyone embraces. Even people who don't attend church and have no real relationship with God are drawn to it. It's because Kings are at work and God is there.

Kings Expand the Kingdom

Most pastors are happy when a new family is added to their congregation. Of course, that is great but Kings expect greater results. They have a right to expect more. They have a Kingdom-way-of-thinking.

Jesus taught us that the Kingdom grows as a mustard seed which starts out small but becomes the largest plant in the garden (Matt. 13:31-32). Seeds grow not just by addition, but exponentially. The

Kingdom of God offers a huge rate of return on investment.

> *"I tell you the truth," Jesus said to them, "no one who has left home or wife or brothers or parents or children for the sake of the kingdom of God will fail to* ***receive many times as much in this age*** *and, in the age to come, eternal life."* (Luke 18:29-30) [Emp. Added]

Kings think in Kingdom terms. They are anointed for it. They carry an anointing not just for a huge return in finances, but in all areas pertaining to the Kingdom of God. Expansion! Multiplication. Exponential growth. They think differently than pastors because they carry a different anointing than pastors. Remember, they are called to expand the Kingdom.

Pastors in the Church, Kings in the Kingdom

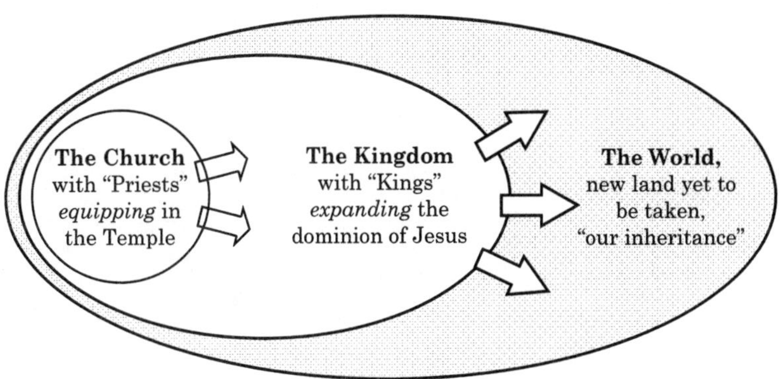

Imagine Discipling Nations

What would happen if we truly believed the words of Jesus?

> *"All authority in heaven and on earth has been given to me. Therefore go and make disciples of all nations, baptizing them in the name of the Father and of the Son and of the Holy Spirit, and teaching them to obey everything I have commanded you. And surely I am with you always, to the very end of the age."*
>
> (Matt. 28:18b-20)

Two thousand years ago, a new King sat down on His throne. He is the King of all kings. He has all authority. He has commissioned His followers to expand His Kingdom. Further, He told them that His Kingdom would grow exponentially. He told them that He would be with them wherever they go.

Imagine being successful in this commission.

Conclusion to Part I

As a bi-vocational pastor, I've dedicated my adult life to growing local churches. I began with a belief that the Church and the Kingdom were the same thing and that we could make disciples and take cities best by planting new local churches. I still believe in local churches. I just don't believe that pastors should be tasked with the burden of city and world evangelism by trying to grow their own churches. It's too big a task for Priests.

We must release the Kings.

Pastors have a priestly anointing for ministries inside the Church. Their job is "equipping of the saints for the work of service..." (Eph. 4:12). Only two percent of the equipped saints can work on staff positions within the Church. The vast majority, 98%, must be sent out to expand the Kingdom of God throughout the world.

Where Do We Go from Here?

The concept of releasing Kings into the marketplace is a remarkable breakthrough that will release the Body of Christ into the "mission" of Christianity—taking the Gospel to the ends of the Earth. Marketplace ministry is an innovative, yet simple, message that can revolutionize people's concepts of ministry and change their understanding of "fruit" to that of reaching the marketplaces of the world.

We could end with this proclamation, except for

one thing—marketplace ministry is not going to happen just because we know it is a good idea. We have to renew our minds. We must change our theology. We need to embrace values which will yield these compelling, kingly motivations.

Every time a new truth comes along, we try it for a while and then watch it wane. We've seen multiple emphases on prayer, evangelism, cell groups, revival, etc. The list goes on but the results are the same—minimal for most of us. The Lord isn't ushering in marketplace ministry merely to be something we do. He's asking us for a different level of relationship at the foundation of our motivation for serving Him. We are going to have to re-examine our concepts of God, our concepts of ourselves, and our views of the future at a fundamental, doctrinal level. We're trading a lifetime of mediocrity for an inheritance beyond all we can ask or think

Why go back to doctrinal foundations for marketplace ministry? Because *working* with God instead of *performing* for Him is fun, addictive, pleasurable, adventurous, joyful, meaningful, and rewarding. Converting from a "religious" to a "relational" motivational base returns us to our first love. You don't have to wait for heaven to experience God's blessings (Psalm 16:11). The Kingdom of God has come upon you (Matt. 12:28).

> *You will show me the path of life;*
> *In Your presence is fullness of joy;*
> *At Your right hand are pleasures forevermore.*
> (Ps. 16:11 NKJV)

Part II
Foundations for Kingly Motivations

Marketplace ministry led by Kings presents us with a radical means to carry out the Great Commission and advance the Kingdom of God. In order for marketplace ministry to take root in our lives, however, our theology (doctrine) needs to undergo some changes.

Most Christians do not take theology very seriously. They are more concerned with real life or "reality." But the fact is that we are all theologians, because we all have a particular theology to which we lean. We carry it with us everywhere we go. We apply it to all kinds of problems, situations, events, and dilemmas. The fact that we don't associate ourselves with those branded as theologians probably means that we never have given our own theology much thought. But whether we ignore it or face it, our theology stands at the center of our being; it affects the way we see everything and our doctrine is at the core of our motivations. Our views of God, our views of ourselves, our views of our neighbors, and our views of our past, present, and future—all are driven by the theological basis which forms the core of our thoughts and motivations.

Marketplace ministry and the role of Kings in advancing the Kingdom of God is based upon key theological concepts in three areas:

1. Who is God?
2. Who is man?
3. What does the future hold?

We cannot grasp firmly and completely the deeper truths of marketplace ministry without an examination of our present theology. We will need to re-orient our thinking as necessary to align fully with the truth embodied in Scripture.

So, let's take this brief journey together. I want to show you some key concepts in your thinking that will release you to living freer and with greater joy. I want to release you into embracing the truths of marketplace ministry. I want you to find your place as Kings, Priests, and Prophets. I want to show you a motivational basis in sound doctrine that will carry you naturally into your destiny.

Chapter 7
Who Is God?

All of us have a picture of God—Who He is and how He acts. It might have been given to us as small children, perhaps from our parents, a Sunday School teacher, or a glossy picture we saw in our grandmother's Bible. Our image of God might have been modified through the years by preachers, books, movies, and TV shows. All of life's joys and triumphs, despairs and tragedies, have helped shaped the image we hold of Him.

That image determines how we relate to God. Therefore, we must be sure that our images of God are correct—accurate according to Scripture.

Most Christians in the Western world do not realize it, but their images of God have been influenced profoundly by Greek philosophy, which lies at the foundation of modern Western thought. Their images have been distorted from that which is revealed in the Bible, and, as a result, they tend to think of God as a huge immoveable force, rather than a Person. Please allow me to explain.

The ancient Greek philosophers (i.e., Plato and Aristotle) attempted to develop an understanding of God using logic apart from the Scriptural revelation. They envisioned a Supreme Being out of Whom Creation emanated, much as light emanates from the sun; however, they reasoned that this Supreme Being must be much, much greater than the sun. He must be the *Prime Mover* of the whole universe.

The ancient Greek philosophers reasoned that if the Prime Mover could push all things into existence, then He was too great to be pushed or moved by that which He created. It is honorable that they saw the greatness of God, but they were left with a sterile force, stoic and unresponsive to His Creation.

This Greek-originated, philosophical concept of God dominated intellectual circles when Christianity began infiltrating the Greek and Roman cultures during the Fourth through Fifth Centuries. Great Church leaders such as Augustine helped the masses embrace many Christian truths, but the immoveable, sterile concept of God remained in the forefront of people's minds. Modern historians refer to it as the "Classical View of God."*

To see how this Classical View seized the minds of Europeans during the Middle Ages, we can think of the huge cathedrals that were constructed. The places where people "met with God" were built with massive stones, reflecting the immovability of God. High lofty ceilings testified of His greatness and distance from the people. The unemotional and stoic concept of God can be seen in how people approached Him within those cathedrals. They typically took on a very quiet, reverent attitude. Since they perceived God to be quiet and "holy," they naturally wanted to take on the same nature when coming into the sanctuary of God.

The Classical View of God continues to influence the minds of people throughout the Western world.

---

* Harold R. Eberle has written a book, entitled, *Who Is God?*, which contrasts the Classical View with the biblical view of God.

Here where I live in the United States, people have been influenced profoundly because they have inherited much from European intellectualism. Even Christians sometimes think of God as a huge cosmic force.

Relating to God as a cosmic force—having no more personality than gravity—is a distortion of God's nature that can leave a Christian enslaved to a life without meaning and fruit. Serving a God who is distant, stoic, and impersonal is frustrating, lonely, and filled with dead works.

"Converting" from knowing God as a *force* to knowing Him *personally* has a number of profound implications in our everyday walk. For Kings to be successful, clear thinking on this issue is essential.

Before I explain what this means for Kings, let me assure you that this is in accordance with the biblical revelation of God. He is interactive, emotional, and personal. He desires to covenant and work with us. He wants to communicate as He did with His people in Bible times.

> *Surely the Sovereign LORD does nothing without revealing his plan to his servants the prophets.* (Amos 3:7)

> *...for the LORD detests a perverse man but takes the upright into his confidence.* (Prov. 3:32)

> *For who has known the mind of the Lord that he may instruct him? But we have the mind of Christ.* (I Cor. 2:16)

God wants to talk to you.

Passivity Turns to Initiative

One characteristic of the Classical View of God is the belief that He has predestined and controls all things.

If, indeed, God orchestrates every detail of our lives, then logically the only thing we can do is align with our predetermined path. Under this view of God, we must be concerned primarily with avoiding rebellion, presumption, and personal ambition—all things that compete with the will of "The Force." Our spiritual disciplines are directed at zeroing out personal initiative so we don't get out of "God's will." Relationship with God is one of "waiting" on Him in the sense of both timing and service. In fact, we spend most of our lives expecting good things and waiting for them to happen. Like a robot, if God doesn't touch the joy stick, we don't make a move. We are left theologically unwilling to take a risk and follow a leading that we might confuse with personal initiative or rebellious ambition.

All of that goes contrary to the nature of Kings. To be a leader you must take initiative. To be at the forefront you must think. To be a King you must act.

The true biblical view of God leads us to believe that He values personal initiative, especially when it springs from a communicating, personal relationship with Him. You do have gifts and talents with which God created you, but how you use them involves some choices that He wants you to make. There is plenty of latitude within the will of God for your initiative to play an important role.

Furthermore, God values the dreams and desires of our hearts as part of His own creative process. He even values our will, because most of the time it is His will, too.

The truth is that as Christians we are His children, His friends, and His co-laborers. He has invited us to be seated with Him in heavenly places and to rule and reign with Him. Our lives have significance. Our prayers really do change the course of future events. This personal, social God really is committed to talking and walking with us.

If God Is Just a Force, I Only Can Know His Principles

At a very deep level, knowing God merely as a force leaves us with no way to relate to Him except by implementing His principles!

Imagine God as a cosmic force. We would know of Him by the principles that He radiates out as sunlight to His people. Just as gravity, He's totally predictable. We're comforted because God is so manageable, predictable, and distant. We try to relate to this God by living out the "Christian" principles in the Bible. If we are performance-oriented anyway, we can be very comfortable with knowing the principles of God and teaching others the same. God becomes impersonal and principled…and so do we.

Those are ingredients that make a poor husband/wife and father/mother. The same ingredients make fruitless Kings or Priests. People don't connect with *principles*; they connect with *people*…and a *personal*

God.

God is personal, social, emotional, and at times, unpredictable. We do have biblical principles but we can't know God through them alone. We have to start talking (and listening) to God. He's not mad at us for trying the principled route. We just don't get directly connected with anything He's doing by implementing principles. At some level, "principled Christians" depend on other Christians to hear God for them. Our lives can be successful on the outside but relationally empty on the inside.

Here are the *"new rules."* We can't predict what God wants. Rules don't buy us much, other than exposing our emptiness and longing for a relationship with a personal God.

> *Wherefore the law was our schoolmaster to bring us unto Christ, that we might be justified by faith. But after that faith is come, we are no longer under a schoolmaster.* (Gal. 3:24-25 KJV)

The principles can tell us when we're out of bounds, but they won't substitute for hearing the voice of God and sensing His leading. We no longer read the Bible for knowledge; we read to hear God speak something into our spirits. When we consider other people who aren't keeping the rules, it's really easy to look past their behavior and see if there isn't some way to connect with them relationally...that's what God did with us!

Kings, such as David, have to connect with a

personal God. The prayer and emotion of the Psalms, the prophetic, the communication with God in the form of questions and answers—all these things become real to us when our doctrine embraces the reality of a personal, relational God.

Principles to Faith

Kings really do live by faith. It's the means by which they are able to get things done in the Kingdom.

However, our approach to the concept of faith also can fall prey to perceiving God as a force and emphasizing His *principles* instead of His *Person.* Many Christians have done this.

You probably have heard—maybe even believed—that faith is the title deed to the promises of God. Once we see a promise in the Bible, we view it as one of the principles of the force and direct our faith toward it and receive; comparable to writing checks on God's account. As long as we keep His principles in obedience, we expect the force to deliver His promises.

The failure point in this approach is relating to a force instead of a personal God. The promises are just the principles of the force and "covenant" is a spiritual sounding word we use to manipulate the force legally. Sounds silly, doesn't it?

Biblical faith occurs after spending time with the Lord and getting the revelation of what He's doing. Once I see what God has in mind, I can step out, act, and even speak the results into existence (Matt.

18:18-20; Mark 11:23). That process is very relational and has little in common with an intellectual approach to finding promises in the Bible and demanding that God do them for us. Notice Jesus' promise for answered prayer ends with the reality that He is "with us".

> *"I tell you the truth, whatever you bind on earth will be bound in heaven, and whatever you loose on earth will be loosed in heaven. Again, I tell you that if two of you on earth agree about anything you ask for, it will be done for you by my Father in heaven. For where two or three come together in my name, there am I with them."* (Matt 18:18-20)

Authority-based Relationships Become Personal Relationships

Most of us have known people in positions of power or influence who were overbearing in their use of authority. What you may not have realized is that there are theological roots in such behavior.

If God is a huge force Who controls everything, we begin to take on the role of an "ant" in the "little-people-big-God" way of relating to Him. As an ant, the focus is on obeying the controlling force in the sense of living by the principles of this great cosmic influence. Smart (or spiritual) ants even may be inclined to learn how to manipulate the force to use it for productive purposes in accordance with their own desires. In any case, we begin to resemble our perception of the God we serve...we become authoritarian, too!

> *The idols of the nations are silver and gold, made by the hands of men....Those who make them will be like them, and so will all who trust in them.*
>
> (Ps. 135:15-18)

Can you see the connection? First, we posture ourselves as ants before a god to make sure we're submissive to his greatness. Next, we treat those under us the same way the god of our false theology treats us. We become what we loathe—authoritarian.

Remember all those arguments in church about authoritarian styles of leadership? Those were not just bad leaders. It was bad theology: people trying to lead others the same way they thought God led them—by the nose.

By contrast, when we begin to relate to the personal God of the Bible, the first thing that happens is that He treats us as His children, destined to be Kings. When that revelation really sinks in, we naturally see other people as God's children...and we treat them as Kings instead of ants. We love them as people instead of minions.

Kings don't "lord over" those they lead. In fact, those with power use it to serve. The style of leadership that Kings are called to use empowers, promotes, and releases the people under them to do "even greater things."

> *Jesus called them together and said, "You know that the rulers of the Gentiles lord it over them, and their high officials exercise authority over them. Not so with you. Instead, whoever wants to become great among you must be your servant, and whoever wants to be first must be your slave—just as the Son of Man did not come to be served, but to serve...."*
>
> (Matt. 20:24-28)

If God Has Emotions, So Should We

Kings might be perceived naturally as "professional" people, neatly dressed, always subdued, controlled, modest, and respectable. Why? Theological roots!

You wouldn't expect to see a cosmic force dancing through the streets, would you? Neither did Plato and his pals. The philosophic concept of God that profoundly has influenced Christianity and the whole Western world was totally void of emotional expression or variation. Since we want to be as God, we value stoicism and show no emotion. Emotions are for the weak in heart, and they are frowned upon by this god who never changes his expression.

In reality, the God of the Bible clearly shows emotions: joy, sorrow, anger, jealousy, and delight. When Jesus went through the courts of the Temple and turned over the tables of the money changers, He appeared more as a raging bull than a humble monk.

He reflected the heart of the Father God in that action. God also experiences the emotion of delight in relating to His people.

> *...the LORD will take delight in you....*
> (Is. 62:4)

> *"I will rejoice over Jerusalem and take delight in my people...."* (Is. 65:19)

You need to be as God—and express your emotions.

A lifetime of "stuffing" your emotions will leave you scarred physically, psychologically, and spiritually. Pretending it's godly to be stoic is a mask that has to come off eventually. "Stuffers" become effectively dysfunctional in the workplace and in ministry. Similar to walking landmines, their personal issues explode when stepped upon.

Further, Kings must be free to experience emotions to stay in touch with their intuitive, creative nature. A big part of learning to hear from God is being willing to act on that "still small voice" of the Holy Spirit. Successful Kings are free to follow their "gut feelings."

Lethargy Turns to Passion

Kings are passionate about their initiatives. They have a sense of ownership, excitement, and importance tied to their activities. That passion, or lack of it, has theological roots, too.

If God were a cosmic force, He would radiate out principles of the universe that would land upon people in a purely impartial way. Those who knew about the principles would use them to accomplish things. Those who were ignorant of the principles of the cosmic god would miss out. He would treat everyone exactly the same.

If that were true, then trying to get close to God with a little "initiative" would be similar to "cheating" on your friends. You would be trying to get an upper hand over a fellow ant. It wouldn't be humble and it would violate the philosophically derived idea that god treats everyone the same.

If we think of God as the sun, evenly bathing all people with the same favor, there is little motivation for individuals to try to please Him. On the other hand, if God is responsive to individuals, then there are things people can do to give Him pleasure. More importantly, you can please Him. There are things which you can do to make Him pleased with you.

Here's the reality. God is not an impersonal force. He sees individuals and He responds to them. He rewards those who step out in faith:

> *And without faith it is impossible to please God, because anyone who comes to him must believe that he exists and that he rewards those who earnestly seek him.*
> (Heb. 11:6)

God does things through and for people who seek Him. He gets really excited about people who hunger and thirst after Him (Matt. 5:6) and He promises to meet them (Rev. 3:16).

Furthermore, God is actively seeking people whom He can bless:

> *For the eyes of the Lord range throughout the earth to strengthen those whose hearts are fully committed to him.*
> (II Chron. 16:9)

God is looking for Kings. He wants to engage them. He wants to get involved with them.

Once you understand this about God, you'll be passionate, spirited, competitive (even aggressive) in pursuing Him, working with Him, and pleasing Him. If you touch the heart and desire of God your goals will be directed toward the Person and purposes of God (II Cor. 5:9).

Living in True Covenant with God

Christians with a Classical View of God will say that they have a covenant with God, but they tend to understand a covenant to be a legally-binding contract between them and God. In particular, they think that the covenant is their legal right to get into Heaven. Of course, Jesus Christ is our door to eternal happiness, but the covenant we have with God is much more than a legal contract. It is a *relational commitment.*

In Bible days whenever two parties entered into covenant with one another, they were committing themselves to make decisions together and work through the problems of life with each other. They would share the same friends and enemies. Their possessions would be available to one another. Covenants were seen as inescapable, lifetime relationship commitments.

To see the difference between a legal understanding of covenant and a relational understanding, consider marriage. The marriage covenant is not meant to be a legal arrangement as much as it is a heart commitment of two people to invest their lives in one another. The two are to work with each other, side by side. They are committed to make decisions together and for the benefit of one another.

An excellent example of how God views covenant is seen in His dealings with Abraham. He conferred with Abraham before destroying Sodom and Gomorrah. God said: "Shall I hide from Abraham what I am about to do...?" (Gen. 18:17). Abraham, knowing he had a covenant with God, dared to reason with God: "Wilt You indeed sweep away the righteous with the wicked?" (Gen. 18:23b). God honored His covenant with Abraham and allowed him to enter into the decision-making process.

Compare this with how the marriage covenant is meant to establish a relationship between two people. In my own marriage, I would be wrong to spend any significant amount of money or make a major decision without allowing my wife to be fully involved in the decision-making process. A covenant is a commitment to cooperate and work with each other.

It is only when we embrace this covenant-making

aspect of God's nature that we can understand many of His actions as recorded in the Bible. For example, there are several biblical accounts where we see God express anger with His people. On more than one occasion God allowed His covenant-partner, Moses, the privilege of reasoning with Him and, thus, talking Him out of destroying the people (i.e., Ex. 32:11-14). The fact that God allowed Moses the honor of influencing His actions is directly related to God's covenant-keeping nature.

God is open for dialogue and He can be influenced in His decisions. God is a Covenant-Maker and a Covenant-Keeper. Those who enter into covenant with God are entitled to a deeper relationship with and closer access to Him. God includes His covenant-partners in His purposes, plans, decisions, and actions. He honors them and receives their input on a greater and more intimate level.

What does this mean for Kings? Your Business-Partner has infinite wisdom and He is wealthy. Listen to Him and He will give you good advice. Work with Him and He will open the windows of resources for you. He is on your side. He has made a covenant—sealed with blood—to be there with you.

What about Mistakes?

A covenant entails commitment. God will not leave you. Even if you make mistakes and are unfaithful, He remains faithful (II Tim. 2:13). He will continue to work with you through difficult times.

This is essential for Kings to know. They must

feel the freedom to act boldly and decisively. Sure, they will make mistakes, but they must know that God is not there ready to club them over the head. As a Business-Partner, He never will sue for damages.

If a Christian is steeped in the view of God that holds an image of him as cold, aloof, and controlling, that Christian is too intimidated to risk an action that might result in a "miss." Imagine God having the future all mapped out and never deviating from that plan. Now imagine making a mistake (sinning) and ruining the whole future of the universe. Still want to step out? No thanks.

Even if we sin, He is willing to forgive.

> *If we confess our sins, he is faithful and just and will forgive us our sins and purify us from all unrighteousness.*
>
> (I John 1:9)

Look at God's account of the great people of faith in the Bible (Heb. 11). Their accomplishments are recorded; their failures are not! Why? They were so completely forgiven, pardoned, washed, and purged that their mistakes don't make the record. Although David committed adultery, covered it up, and murdered the defrauded husband, he is counted as a man after God's own heart...centuries after all his mistakes!

> *"I have found David son of Jesse a man after my own heart; he will do everything I want him to do."* (Acts 13:22)

Not only is there forgiveness for those who repent, but we have the perfect Business-Partner. He has the ability to undo the consequences of our mistakes.

> *And we know that all things work together for good to them that love God, to them who are the called according to his purpose.* (Rom. 8:28 KJV)

Yes, this God is powerful and He will help us straighten out the greatest of messes.

Kings do make mistakes—probably more than others—because decisions are made in greater numbers and significance. We would wilt if God didn't pardon us and remove the guilt, shame, and even the consequences of making mistakes. We serve a God who is personal, powerful, forgiving, and has the ability to make adjustments.

Praise His name! Sign on the dotted line, now.

God Is Our Father

Finally, we must see God as our Father.

If He is truly a Father, then He must have desires for us much as a human father has for his sons and daughters. A father desires his children to be healthy, happy, and successful in life. The overriding dynamic in the relationship is for a father to help his children rise and become all they can be. If God is, indeed, a Father, then His predominant desire must be for us to *rise, be happy, and be successful.*

In contrast, if God is a cosmic, impersonal force, then He has no real desire for our success. He can take it or leave it. He is unaffected by our struggles or daily affairs.

If God is a Father to you, then you are His child. You have immeasurable value to Him. Even if you sin, He will welcome you back into His arms comparable a father who longs for his prodigal son. He is watching. He cares. Everything you do has value.

As a father, what do I want for my children? I want them to mature and succeed. When they were young, my wife and I exercised much authority in their lives. Now that they are older, we want to help and bless them, giving them guidance when they seek it. I still want them to love and honor me, but most of all I want them to discover their own paths in life. I want them to have my nature and my values. Yet, I want them to think and act on their own. By God's grace, I hope they will do the things that I would do if I were in their positions. But I also want them to go beyond what I would do.

Of course, I hope my children always will communicate with me because I still want to be involved in their lives. But whether or not they telephone me, I love them and I want them to be happy.

Chapter 8
Who Am I?

If God is my Father, then I am His child.

I am not just an ant trying to eke out an existence on this planet. I am significant. In fact, I have been born into a kingly and priestly family. I can rule over the affairs of life. I have access to God.

If I have a covenant with God, then I have the Most Supreme Partner. He is wise and wealthy. If I work with Him, than I am bound to be successful.

If God—the Creator of the universe—is working with me and I am created in His image, then I can be creative. With His breath in me, I will have His thoughts and His perspective. I will have energy to rise above the problems of life. I will have innovative ideas that haven't yet occurred to anyone else. I will ask Him, and He may give to me ways to expand His Kingdom into business, government, and every area of society in which He desires to express Himself and establish His rulership.

If I am created in God's image, then I have a mind that can conceive, a heart that can dream, and a spirit that can soar. If God is with me, the limits are off and the future is open.

The Battlefield of Theology

All of our positive thoughts come to a screeching halt when confronted by certain theological teachings which are common in some Christian circles today. The teaching which I will challenge here is the one that says people are totally depraved, having nothing good within their natures. Millions of Christians hold to this doctrine. They live with deep suspicions that everyone around them is evil to the core. Furthermore, they think of themselves and other Christians as sinners—bad people—saved by grace.

Please do not misunderstand me. I believe that all people sin. I believe we all need a Savior who is Jesus Christ. I believe in the redeeming work of God. I proclaim to all that we only can be saved by grace when we put our faith in Jesus Christ.

What I do *not* believe is that non-Christians are totally evil. Further, I do not believe that Christians should think of themselves as sinners. Of course, we all sin, but that must not be the focus of our attention. Christians must realize that they are children of God. Furthermore, we must recognize that even non-Christians are created in God's image, and they have many positive characteristics.

A Christian businesswoman who thinks of herself as a contemptible sinner cannot step out in confidence. If she gets a great idea to start a new business project, thoughts will leap into her mind that she is not worthy. If she plans to accept a new endeavor, she will be shocked into paralysis by the shouting doubts that she has reviewed so often:

> "Wait a minute! I am a sinful creature, am I not? There can be no good in me, apart from the presence of God."

Once such thoughts seize her mind, she is left helpless. Creative thoughts disappear. Initiative is gone. If she is riddled with doubts about her own nature, she never will be confident enough to do what she has been created and called by God to do.

The Christian who is chained to doctrinal beliefs of the evilness of all humanity never will reach out to his neighbor successfully. He may offer some token conversation and feign the interest of a good neighbor, but he consciously and subconsciously will erect a huge fence to protect himself from the evil human being living next door.

A Christian factory owner never will trust his banker, his accountant, or partner. He won't take his watchful eyes off of his receptionist, secretary, or assistant. Each employee must be treated as a slave who needs to be controlled, rather than as a human being worthy of respect.

If we believe that people are rotten to the core, barely saved by grace, then insecurities within will cry out for God to take control of everything, leaving us with nothing to do but be slaves ourselves.

In the face of terrible thoughts about oneself and others, a Christian never can be effective in marketplace ministry. Until we resolve certain theological issues about our own natures and roles in life, we never will rise into our roles as Kings and Priests.

Our Theological Roots

From where do such negative thoughts about humanity come? Bad theology.

During the Third to Fifth Centuries, most Church leaders began accepting the doctrine that all people are inherently evil. Augustine was perhaps the most influential in this, but he reasoned that evil was released into babies as they were conceived because of the sexual passion aroused in their parents.

The idea that people are basically bad or sinful from birth became soundly seated in Protestant Christianity by Reformers such as Luther and Calvin. In their attempts to bring the Church to understand justification by faith, they emphasized the sinfulness of all humanity. Certainly these Church leaders had good intentions, and they were instrumental in bringing the Church out of the Dark Ages. But they thought of people as totally depraved, having nothing good in them.

I don't wish to cast the slightest doubt on our Christian heritage and I do believe that every human being sins. However, I want to re-examine some Bible passages to find a balance concerning these issues.*

People are Precious

Is it true that people are naturally evil to the core before salvation? Is it true that the only good people are those who are saved?

Scripture clearly refers to many unsaved people as good.

Now there was a man named Joseph, a

---

* In his book, *Precious in His Sight*, Harold R. Eberle more fully discusses these issues related to the nature of humanity.

member of the Council, a good and upright man.... (Luke 23:50-51)

Note that Joseph was not a Christian. He was a Jew, and yet the Bible refers to him as "good" (from the Greek word, *agathos*).

In another passage, a Gentile named Cornelius is referred to in this way:

He and all his family were devout and God-fearing.... (Acts 10:2)

Here is a man who was not yet saved, and yet he is called "devout and God-fearing."

Then there are the words of Jesus referring to both good and evil people.

"The good man brings good things out of the good stored up in him, and the evil man brings evil things out of the evil stored up in him." (Matt. 12:35)

Jesus would not have said this if good people did not exist.

Certainly, the Bible differentiates between the goodness of man and the goodness of God. As Jesus said when someone called Him "good teacher":

"Why do you call me good?" Jesus answered. "No one is good—except God alone." (Mark 10:18)

Here, Jesus is making a statement about the goodness of humanity compared with the goodness of God. In that comparison, the goodness of God is perfection, something that no human being can attain on his/her own. However, in a less strict sense we can say that certain people are good.

That does not mean they are saved apart from the work of Jesus Christ. Of course, not. Everyone sins. We all need a Savior. Even good people sin from time to time.

But the point is that the Bible and Jesus Himself referred to good people.

Evil by Our Inherited Nature?

The belief that all people are totally evil has held millions of Christians in chains for generations. It changes how we view everything: ourselves, our neighbors, the workings of society, the future, and ministry to the unsaved.

Several Scriptures commonly are misinterpreted to support the belief that people are inherently evil. For example, Paul wrote:

> *Therefore, just as sin entered the world through one man, and death through sin, and in this way death came to all men, because all sinned.* (Rom. 5:12)

Note carefully what the Bible is teaching here. When Adam fell, sin entered "the world" (*kosmos*, in the Greek). It does not say that sin entered the inherited nature of humanity. Sin entered the world. Hence, in this world there is evil and temptations do exist. Indeed, all people yield to the power of sin during their lives, but that does not mean they are born with totally evil natures which were passed on to them from Adam.

Our Righteousness Is Not Filthy Rags

Another commonly misinterpreted Scripture is from Isaiah:

> *All of us have become like one who is unclean, and all our righteous acts are like filthy rags....* (Is. 64:6)

Taken out of context, this Scripture seems to be saying that all of a person's attempts at righteousness are filth. However, this Scripture is not speaking about all of humanity. It refers to the Jews during a particularly difficult time in their history. To see that there were also good Jewish people, look at the verse preceding it:

> *You come to the help of those who gladly do right, who remember your ways....* (Is. 64:5)

There are those who "gladly do right." They are the standard by which the writer was judging the present group of people who were not doing right. This judgment is not against all people, but against a select group of Jews who had fallen from righteousness.

Sinful from Birth?

David's lament in the following verse is also used by many to conclude that people are sinful from birth.

> *Behold, I was shapen in iniquity; and in sin did my mother conceive me.*
> (Ps. 51:5 KJV)

In reality, it is a mistake to take one Scripture such as this one and build a doctrine that encompasses all of humanity. Many scholars attribute David's cry of a sinful origin to his birth being illegitimate, a concept supported by other factors in his life.*

In other Bible passages King David made comments which sound very positive concerning his relationship to God from birth. For example:

> *Yet you brought me out of the womb; you made me trust in you even at my mother's breast. From birth I was cast upon you; from my mother's womb you have been my God.* (Ps. 22:9-10)

Compare these words with the words of Paul and Jeremiah who both talked about being set apart for

* For further teaching on all of these subjects see, *Precious in His Sight,* by Harold R. Eberle.

God at or before birth.

> *But when God, who set me apart from birth and called me by his grace....*
> (Gal. 1:15)

> *"Before I formed you in the womb I knew you, before you were born I set you apart; I appointed you as a prophet to the nations."* (Jer. 1:5)

Children are not born evil. Of course, everyone sins during his/her lifetime. We all fall to temptation. We all need a Savior. However, we are not corrupt from birth.

None Righteous?

Probably the Scripture most widely used to teach that people are totally evil is taken from Romans, chapter three:

> *There is no one righteous, not even one; there is no one who understands, no one who seeks God. All have turned away, they have together become worthless; there is no one who does good, not even one.* (Rom. 3:10-12)

Just as the verse in Isaiah, this verse often is taken out of context in order to teach the worthless, evil nature of humanity.

Look again at Romans 3:12 and notice how that people "turned away" and "became worthless." This presumes that they were on the right track at first and that sin derailed them. They were drawn into a sinful state of their own free wills.

In the first two chapters of Romans, people are seen as having a natural awareness of God's existence and a willingness to obey Him.

> *(Indeed, when Gentiles, who do not have the law, do by nature things required by the law, they are a law for themselves, even though they do not have the law, since they show that the requirements of the law are written on their hearts, their consciences also bearing witness, and their thoughts now accusing, now even defending them.)* (Rom. 2:14-15)

"By nature" many Gentiles do the things required by the Law. They have some natural consciousness of right and wrong. Many non-Christians do many good things.

Reaching "Good People" Who Aren't Saved

If we believe that people are basically evil, we view others darkly, with suspicion and even loathing. On the other hand, if we believe that people are basically good, albeit with a vulnerability toward sin, then we view them vastly differently. Believing that people are created in God's image, we tend to look for good in them. We then expect good from what others do, and we feel confident in our own ability to convey good in return.

The unsaved world—those unacquainted with Jesus Christ as Savior—can perceive our attitudes toward them. When they sense that we believe they are evil, then, quite naturally and understandably, they are going to withdraw. The fact that many Christian testimonies of salvation involve stories of horrendous travesty before reaching the saving knowledge of Christ is evidence of the excessive qualifications that evangelicals place on any who would be converted. Many require that they accept the fact that they are evil before being allowed to apply the blood of Jesus Christ to their lives and enter a salvation relationship with God.

The message of total human depravity does nothing to reach those unsaved people that lead productive lives and haven't fallen into the depths of sin. The homemaker who feels a deep longing for a spiritual sense of belonging yearns for something eternal. The businessperson who works honestly and diligently, wonders at the end of the day if there is something more—something worth fighting for, something more than just earning a living. The scientist yearns for knowledge, reaching into the unknown as far as her learning can take her, wondering what or who will be on the other side of the frontier she is reaching. All these people, and countless more, need God. And yet they live decent, functional lives. They go to work, feed their families, care for their young, look out for the elderly, and work to make society a better place in which to live. They pay their taxes, obey the law, and walk in relatively straight paths. Some, such as policemen, firefighters, and soldiers, even give their lives for the privileges that we have in this blessed world.

The portion of the Church which believes in total depravity has a focus on reaching the "down and outers." But, in reality that message precludes us from reaching "normal people" who don't happen to be consumed by sin and its consequences. Marketplace ministry seeks to reach these people, but it will not succeed with a false concept of humanity's total depravity. We will reach them with the message of God's love. We will reach them with the Gospel of Jesus Christ.

What Do We Really Believe?

What do we really think of the unchristian world? Certainly, prevailing doctrine presents one position, but what do our actions say? Do we really believe that the non-Christians are totally evil? When we put our children on the school bus, is the driver a Christian? When we visit the doctor, is the doctor saved? When we enter the highways, are the majority of drivers who are aiming their cars within a few feet of ours, believers? If we truly believe that our non-Christian fellowman is totally evil, why do we trust our families, our safety, our very lives to these people?

The truth is, we don't believe it, not really. We know there is good in most people and we trust that good in them. When we need our teeth fixed, we don't insist that the dentist is a Christian; instead we want a good dentist. When we need a prescription filled, we count on the pharmacy staff to know what they are doing. When the mechanic fixes our car, we don't ask if he is a Christian, although we may pray for him and wish he'd take that calendar down from his garage wall. But we pay him for his good work and drive away in confidence. If we are really honest with ourselves, we will offer up a prayer of thanksgiving to God for the blessings of good people in this world and pray that they enter into a relationship with their loving God.

WORK – The Final Frontier

Marketplace ministry seeks to reach the hearts and minds of people before sin can erode their ability to know the difference between good and evil. It is an outreach to those who are doing good in their own right. It is an outreach to people where they live and work. It reaches to the place where most of our relationships are made, where our spouses frequently are found, where we experience much of our growth, and where we derive the means to do all that is in our hearts. Marketplace ministry reaches people where they work and live.

People at work are usually at their best, putting forth their best. The cares of life, their own shortcomings, their fears and needs, all are put aside temporarily while the task at hand becomes the sole focus of the person. The man behind the counter at the local burger joint is not there to focus on his broken relationship with his girlfriend. From the time that he puts on his paper hat, he is there to serve food to customers. His thoughts of his lost sweetheart may run in the background, but his focus is primarily on something other than himself or his problems. He is pushing out fries, shakes, and sandwiches to the hungry mob, and, chances are, he is doing it well. If he were not doing it well, he would not be there for long.

Please note that phrase: "doing it well." The person who takes you into the dentist's chair, lays you back, and cleans your teeth, may have reached a crisis in her life the night before, but while you are in her care, her attention is on you. She is putting forth her best. She is giving you the attention that you need, and your teeth are the better for it.

Everywhere in the marketplace, people start their days by showering, brushing their teeth, putting on clean clothes, and hurrying to arrive on time. Why? Because they fear getting fired? No. What primarily motivates people to come to work everyday is the joy and satisfaction of making a difference...of helping somebody else...of making this world a little better...of changing the world, one day at a time.

Marketplace ministry recognizes that the majority of these honest, hardworking people need to be reached for the Kingdom. They need God and they are the next generation of Kings.

These people are alienated by invitations to Christianity that start with: "Come to Jesus, you wretched, evil sinner." While the majority of people know that something is missing in their lives, they do not think of themselves as wretched, evil sinners. They simply do not. How do we know? Talk with them. Listen to them. Work with them. People simply do not think of themselves as evil. They think of themselves as somebody who needs God, a God they cannot fully imagine, a God Who they sense loves them, a God Who loved them enough to send His Son so that they could have a relationship with Him.

> *"For God so loved the world that he gave his one and only Son, that whoever believes in him shall not perish but have eternal life."* (John 3:16)

Note what God loved: the world.

When was the last time you heard an altar call sounding like this?

> "Come unto me, you engineers and scientists, you teachers and musicians, you tireless mothers and fathers, nurses and doctors, you workers and laborers. Lay your shovels, brushes, calculators, computers, chalk, and stethoscopes on the altar and surrender your lives to the God of Creation. Recognize the redemptive work of Jesus Christ, the blood He shed on the Cross, and His life-giving resurrection. Allow God to establish a relationship with you, and then go, pick up your instruments and go back to work. Build sanitation facilities, develop

> new medicines, teach in the schools, build great factories, lead your children to God, and reach out to the world."

Churches with a negative view of humanity miss the majority of normal, hardworking people. Why? Why can't we harness this army of professionals and send them forth to advance the Kingdom of God? We can't send them because we haven't reached them. We've tried to reach them with a flawed Gospel that said they were totally evil, when they really weren't. We tried to teach them the same tired lines about conformity and wretchedness and abandonment to evil ways, and they ignored us. They know better. They passed us by and went to tend to their children, care for their loved ones, and prepare for their next day in the marketplace. They did not listen to us because they were busy serving people, developing better ways of doing things, and improving the standard of living for all of us.

A Theology for Personal Initiative

We really were created in God's own image. He made us much as Himself so we could fellowship with Him. We have similar emotions, desires, dreams...we think as God because He made us that way. The fact that people sin and need forgiveness isn't the whole story. When we think about work associates (saved and unsaved), we must see them as precious to God. They really are generous, helpful, polite, hard-working, creative, fun-loving, and delightful. Sure, they have some quirks, too. A few wear their dysfunctions on their sleeves. But we need to help all people get through life successfully because that is what Jesus would do.

We are a lot happier when we see people the way God does—as precious, but flawed. They often are hurting and need forgiveness, but God has those answers. Since we're created in His image, He's given us many of those answers as ambassadors to His creatures. They get healed when we pray for them. We can see their hurts and get the sense of their callings and giftings. We can love them.

It's easy to see why God values people and how He relates to and works with them. They really are treasures in earthen vessels. We see how God could entrust them with anointing, influence, authority, and wealth to minister to others. We can see how God's people can be creative and call on the resources of Heaven and bring new ideas, and answers, and resources into being. Now we understand that God not only permits us to take initiative, He expects us to. It's one of our God-like qualities.

Chapter 9
What Is in the Future?

Finally, we need to look at a Christian's view of the future and its impact on marketplace ministry. If we accept that God is a remote, all-knowing, all-controlling Deity Who requires obedience as the highest honor we can give, and if we further accept that we are inherently evil to the core, then our view of the world's future will be skewed seriously toward fatalism, destruction, and darkness. However, with a clear understanding of what the Bible is really teaching about the nature of God and the nature of humanity, we can clear out our misconceptions of tragic endtime predictions and see the future as Scripture reveals it.

Your Eschatology

"Eschatology" is the theological term for the study of endtime events. Millions of American Christians have learned their eschatology from certain engaging preachers and televangelists who teach that everything is predetermined down to the tiniest detail, leaving nothing for us to do but watch the unfolding events before us. Those events include Satan progressively taking over the minds of non-Christians; an evil individual called the Antichrist taking total control of the finances and governments of this world; a Great Tribulation lasting seven years, during which time God will pour out His wrath upon the Earth, ending in destruction which encompasses all of humanity's existence: economic, political, social, physical, and spiritual. All fronts will be subjected to the most nefarious afflictions ever known. At some point (before, during, or after the Tribulation), God will remove Christians from the Earth by "rapturing" them into Heaven. All of this could occur at any moment and it most likely will happen very soon.

I will refer to this eschatological viewpoint as "modern, fear-based eschatology" because Bible teachers studied in these areas recognize this way of thinking as a recent phenomenon in the Church and originating from a very pessimistic perspective (in comparison to the optimistic perspective which I will explain shortly).

Here are some of the key implications of modern, fear-based eschatology, followed by a diagram that depicts the persecuted, ineffective, and soon-to-be raptured Church.

- The **world** is getting darker and darker, while humanity is becoming increasingly degenerate to the point that God soon will have to pour out His wrath and destroy everything.
- **Governments** and nations are more and more becoming evil tools of the Antichrist. Christians must be particularly leery of Russia, and China (they are Gog and Magog referred to in Scripture), or any coalition of nations which try to work together, such as the United Nations or the European Economic Union.

- The **Church** is an ark on a stormy sea, strong in herself, but impotent to change the evil which is flooding this world. We dare not leave the protection of the Church lest we be left behind.
- The **message** of the Church is to preach the Gospel to all nations, but don't expect a response from a generally evil population. In fact, a great apostasy will come in the future. At best, a faithful remnant will make it through successfully.
- The **Kingdom of God** is something which is up in Heaven right now, and Jesus will bring it to the Earth for a 1,000-year period after the Tribulation. Hence, the Kingdom is not to be experienced today and any attempt to establish the reign of Jesus Christ now is vain.
- **Work** is a necessary evil, a curse, that contaminates us with worldly influences.

The Worldview of Christians Holding to Modern, Fear-based Eschatology

The Consequences of Your Eschatology

If a believer holds to the views of the modern, fear-based eschatology, can you expect him/her to be effective in the marketplace? The practical and theological answer is a simple, "NO."

Imagine a businessperson sitting in Church on Sunday morning listening to the preacher try to convince him/her that the Antichrist will soon take over all finances and economic control. Furthermore, God, at any moment, is going to burn everything. How can that shell-shocked businessperson go to work Monday morning, plan for the future, hire new employees, or develop products and marketing plans? How can a teacher, who believes the world is about to end, teach mathematics, science, English, and other subjects which never will be useful to the students sitting in the classroom? How can a newly married couple invest in a home or plan for a family when their pastor tells them week after week that everything is about to end?

Too many Christians carry a fear-based worldview that is robbing them of faith, hope, and love. They have accepted the lie that the Church is impotent and never will impact this world in any significant way. Their perception is stealing their hope because they see the Church as a cumbersome ark moving through an ocean of evil. They focus on the myth that Satan is in control of this world, rather than recognizing that Jesus is Lord and Satan already has been defeated. They think that they love people, but in reality, they live with abiding suspicions that their neighbor, the government, the church across town, the financial giants, Russia, China, and the Islamic world soon will be used by the Antichrist to deceive all those who are unaware.

Modern, fear-based eschatology leads one to believe that somewhere there are evil leaders now meeting and strategizing how they will take over the world—if they have not taken control already. An evil conspiracy is in progress.

I have good news for you. I have an optimistic eschatology to offer you. There is only one conspiracy that will end in the takeover of this Earth. It is a holy conspiracy. Jesus Christ and the Church are in the process of taking control. God is answering our prayers: "Thy Kingdom come, Thy will be done on Earth as it is in Heaven." The Kingdoms of this world are becoming the Kingdoms of our God. The Kingdom of God was established 2,000 years ago when Jesus sat down on His throne, and the Kingdom is growing as seeds in good soil. Yes, there is a great conspiracy to take over the world. I am a part of it and I hope you are, too.

The Historic Church Had a Victorious View

You should know that the pessimistic teachings of modern, fear-based eschatology have been popular in Christianity for only the past 50 years—and in truth those teachings are originating primarily from a small area in the world, in particular segments of mistaken Christian groups in the United States.

Most of the historic Church around the world for

the last 2,000 years has held a victorious outlook, believing that it is our job to establish the Kingdom of God (that is the will of Jesus Christ) over this Earth. Furthermore, we shall be successful in this task. To see this, just think of the Church during the Middle Ages and the huge cathedrals that were built. Many of those cathedrals took more than 100 years to construct. The people were not thinking that Jesus Christ might return at any moment. No. They were taking responsibility to establish the Church for generations to come.

The most common eschatological belief in the Church during the last 2,000 years is called "Amillennialism," a belief which emphasizes that it is the Church's responsibility to establish the Kingdom of God here on this Earth now. I am not espousing Amillennialism, but I do embrace the God-given responsibility we have to establish the Kingdom of God here on Earth while we are alive. I also want to make you aware of how other Christians in history and across the world believe. Amillennialism remains, even today, the primary eschatological belief of most of the mainline denominations, such as Lutheran, Methodist, Presbyterian, Anglican, Roman Catholic, and Orthodox.

Many of my readers may have rejected the beliefs of "old mainline denominations" because they consider themselves to be more "biblically based." If you are one of them, you also should know that the vast majority of Christians in America who considered themselves as "Bible-believing" throughout the 1800's held to "Postmillennial eschatology," which is a view even more victorious than Amillennialism. Historians often recognize the Postmillennial beliefs of Christians in the 1800's as the impetus for many positive societal changes during the nineteenth century, including the founding of many universities.

The views of modern, fear-based eschatology are a relatively recent phenomena within Christianity. As a Bible-believing Christian, I have rejected those views. I hope that you, too, will reexamine the Scriptures. I really do not care how you envision all of the end time details working out, so long as you embrace the hope of a victorious Church and advancing Kingdom.*

The Truth Will Set You Free

Can you see the importance of changing your worldview? How productive can you be if you believe that God is merely a Force, people are totally evil, and the future is bleak because God's wrath soon will be poured out on all this world? Can you see the impact that modern, fear-based eschatology has on you and on marketplace ministry?

The function of Kings is to advance the Kingdom of God through the marketplace. That kind of outreach takes forethought, planning, and most of all, an optimistic view of the future. No one with a pessimistic view of an impending destruction is going to try very hard to reach the lost through marketplace ministry.

---

* For a full presentation of a victorious eschatology see Harold R. Eberle's book entitled *Bringing the Future into Focus*, available through Worldcast Publishing, Yakima, WA.

Under this dark teaching, the average Christian will go into a holding pattern. Indeed, today there are Christians who won't plan for retirement or save for their children's education because they feel that a rapture is right around the corner. Others who are gifted in politics and government excuse themselves from running for office with the idea that it's all going to be over soon—so why bother? Many Christians look forward to the world suffering mightily in the Tribulation, while they observe it from the safety of the clouds. These are seriously flawed attitudes, and they are holding back the advancement of the Kingdom of God.

The truth is that the Kingdom of God is advancing. Jesus is Lord. And we are victorious here on this Earth. Try going to work tomorrow with that attitude!

Things Are Getting Better

Any serious study of history will reveal that the world is not getting darker and darker, but rather improving. Yes, there are pockets of resistance and evil unspeakable in some dark corners. Indeed, we still have major battles ahead of us, but an honest appraisal of world history will lead to the conclusion that, generally speaking, things are getting better.

Just take a couple of snapshots back in time. For example, as an American citizen I can glance back 200 years and see the conditions of my country in the early 1800's. There were some godly leaders laying the foundation of our government but the moral and ethical climate of America was tragic. The enslavement of tens of thousands of Africans was a curse upon our culture. Thousands of Chinese people also were being brought into our country to serve as forced laborers. Several of our early presidents owned slaves. President Jefferson is known to have fathered several children through his slaves. The native Americans were being forced off of their lands and many murdered. Pioneers who pushed into the West had almost no churches to attend until years after their settlements were established. Church membership records of that time reveal that the percentage of US citizens attending church then was smaller than it is today. The age of sexual consent in some states was 13 years old. History books tell us that alcoholism was at its highest rate in our country's history. Things were not better morally, ethically, nor spiritually at that time in our history. The "good old days" were not so good.

Glance back further and take a snapshot of the whole world 2000 years ago. When Jesus Christ came into this world as a baby, the Jews were the only group of people in the whole world that had a revelation of the one true God—and even they had not recognized the Messiah. They lived under the domination of Greek culture and the Roman government, both people groups who worshipped many gods, such as Zeus and Venus. At that time in history, most Africans and North Americans were worshipping their ancestors or elements of nature itself. Similarly, the millions in China, India, Russia, and Australia were wandering in darkness. In South

America, millions were worshipping a bloodthirsty god who demanded human sacrifices, often numbering in the thousands in one ceremony.

Do you think the world was better 2000 years ago? Think again. Consider the words of Paul when he reminded the early Christians of their previous condition: "...formerly you who are Gentiles...were separate from Christ...without hope and without God in the world." (Eph. 2:11-12).

So many Christians today have bought into the everything-is-going-downhill message. When the television brings news of some tragic event to their attention, they lose sight of the bigger picture. They forget that Christianity is exploding in growth across the world today. According to current growth trends, the Church will triple in size between 2000 and 2010. Right now the greatest growth is happening in China, with 20,000 to 25,000 Chinese becoming Christians every day. The same television that brings bad news is now broadcasting the Gospel to every corner of the Earth for the first time in history.

If you have been seduced by modern, fear-based eschatology, then your eyes will be focused on the evils which, indeed, do remain in the Earth. On the other hand, if you have done any real study of world history, you will be glad that you are alive today, rather than at any previous time in history.

Progressive Eschatology

I hold to what is called "Progressive Eschatology." Jesus Christ will build His Church (His people) and the gates of hell will not prevail against it (Matt. 16:18). The Kingdom of God is growing and it will continue to grow until it is the largest tree in the garden (Matt. 13:31-32). Of course, there will be struggles between righteousness and unrighteousness until Jesus returns, but the greatest revival which the world ever has seen is ahead of us.

Here are some of the key implications of progressive eschatology, followed by the diagram which we have been using throughout this book, showing the Church and the Kingdom of God growing across the Earth.

- The **world** is getting brighter and brighter as the glory of the Lord is progressively being revealed.
- **Governments,** nations, and leaders are tools in God's hand. His government is increasing (Is. 9:6) and the authority structures or nations that exist are established by God (Rom. 13:1). We have a responsibility as Kings to possess the lands of politics and governments.
- The **Church** is becoming a spotless Bride, a demonstration of God's glory, power, and love.
- The **message** of the Gospel is being preached to the world, and we are making disciples of all nations (Matt. 28:19-20).
- The **Kingdom of God** is accessible now for Christians, and it is advancing in the world to influence the marketplace and all areas of society.
- **Work** is a blessing and a calling from God. My occupation is where ministry occurs.

The Worldview of Progressive Eschatology *

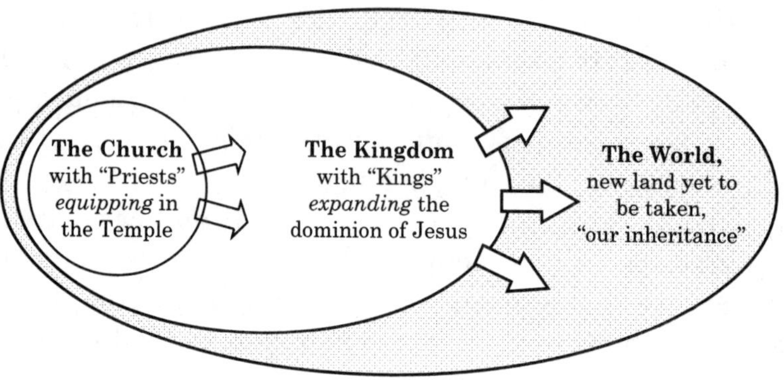

* For a complete explanation of Progressive Eschatology, consult *Bringing the Future into Focus*, by Harold R. Eberle. (www.worldcastpublishing.com)

Conclusion to Part II

We have considered essential theological adjustments that will provide a natural motivation for marketplace ministry. We have set about to embrace a personal God, show a realistic view of humanity, and provide an optimistic basis for the future.

Do you believe these things? Whether or not you accept them, it is vital that you look into your own theology and uncover your own beliefs. Your entire life is motivated by your view of God, humanity, and the future. I encourage you to examine the material carefully, do further reading, come to your own conclusions.

With an eschatology of optimism as a motivetional foundation, we can move "naturally" into marketplace ministry and release a generation of Kings to help us carry out the Great Commission of expanding God's Kingdom into all the Earth.

Part III
Attributes of Kings, Motivated for the Marketplace

Kings have accepted their responsibility to manage the family business.

What is the *family business*? The Earth. Politics. Humanity. Economics. Agriculture. Arts. Communication. Life on this planet. God commissioned people to:

> *"Be fruitful and increase in number; fill the earth and subdue it...."* (Gen. 1:28)

He wants us to manage the affairs of this planet in peace and righteousness. He desires us to produce an abundance.

It is a *family* business. Kings realize that they are not merely slaves, but sons and daughters of God. They are not just living in obedience, but are family members taking responsibility for the Father's business.

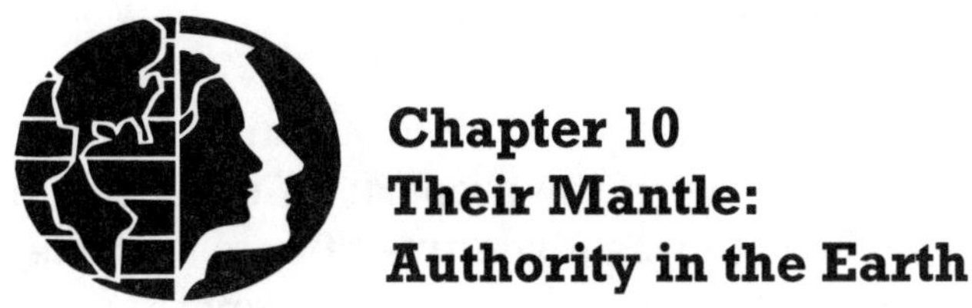

Chapter 10
Their Mantle: Authority in the Earth

God made men and women in His image to rule and subdue the Earth—to be fruitful and fill it.

> *What is man that you are mindful of him, the son of man that you care for him? You made him a little lower than the heavenly beings and crowned him with glory and honor. You made him ruler over the works of your hands; you put everything under his feet:* (Ps. 8:4-6)

God is looking for people to rule and reign with Him.

Do you see, then, how important your eschatology is? If you, as a Christian, think of the Church as God's only ark, drowning in an ocean of evil, an ocean that God soon will destroy, why would you be concerned about preserving, managing, and improving the Earth? Many Christians have fallen for the worldview that our only responsibility is within the four walls of the church. They have abandoned the secular world to non-Christians. Their theology has left them hiding, impotent, unconcerned, and irresponsible.

Is this Earth really our responsibility? Yes. God owns it. Satan tried to steal it. Jesus came to take it back. It is now under His authority. But He has put us in charge.

Our Lord Jesus told a parable about three men who were entrusted with the property of their master (Matt. 25:14-28). One was given five talents of money, another was given two talents, and another one talent. The first man with five talents invested his money wisely and made five more. The second used his two talents to gain two more. But the third man hid his talent for fear that he might lose it. Then when the master came back, he demanded his servants to give an account concerning what they had done with their talents. The two who increased their wealth were praised and put in charge of even greater blessings. The third man was rebuked and punished by his master.

This parable was told to instruct us about our responsibilities while we are here. God will hold us accountable to use whatever He has given to us. Fear causes us to hide. Faith causes us to rise up and do great things. On judgment day we each will stand before our God and give an account concerning what we have done with our talents.

The King of kings has commissioned us to establish His Kingdom. In fact, we are co-rulers with Him:

> *And God raised us up with Christ and seated us with him in the heavenly realms in Christ Jesus.* (Eph. 2:6)

We go out to the nations from a position of victory. We are Kings.

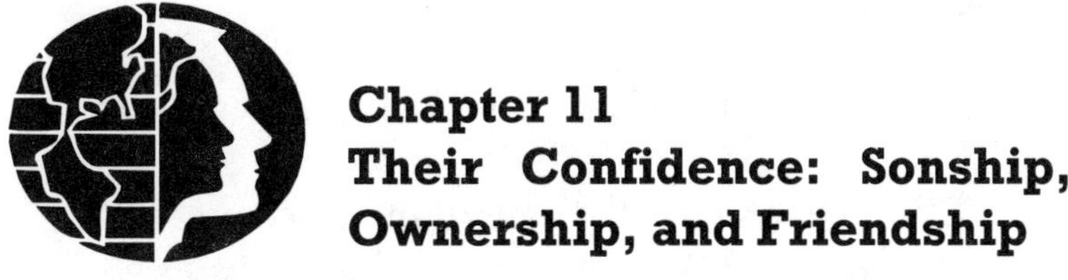

Chapter 11
Their Confidence: Sonship, Ownership, and Friendship

As Kings, we are establishing the Kingdom of our Father. We are His sons.

Hopefully, we have grown to embrace our responsibilities.

> *What I am saying is that as long as the heir is a child, he is no different from a slave, although he owns the whole estate. He is subject to guardians and trustees until the time set by his father. So also, when we were children, we were in slavery....So then you are no longer a slave, but a son; and since you are a son, God has made you also an heir.*
>
> (Gal. 4:1-7)

An heir owns things. To keep those things, he must embrace the responsibilities of ownership.

Someone who owns his own home acts differently than a renter or a squatter. A squatter does not care about the condition of the shelter in which he illegally resides. He uses and abuses it. A renter only does the required maintenance. An owner paints, landscapes, and improves the value of the home.

We are owners not just of a home, but of a family business. The previous business Owner is staying on as our Partner. We can go to Him and receive counsel, direction, and instruction. He is a Friend.

> *"I no longer call you servants, because a servant does not know his master's business. Instead, I have called you friends, for everything that I learned from my Father I have made known to you."* (John 15:15)

Kings Undergo an "Identity Shift"

When a son takes over the family business, he acts much differently than an employee. He takes responsibility. He acts not as a slave, waiting for every order to come from above, but he initiates business. He originates new ideas and ways to advance the business. He engages his energy, passion, and life into all that is set before him.

The Bible uses a number of metaphors to describe our relationship with God. While not discounting any of them, we can observe a progression toward *relationship* as shown in the diagram below. Each of the terms has a biblical application to our lives. However, God is drawing us to be involved in His family business; drawing us to relate to Him in a much closer way.

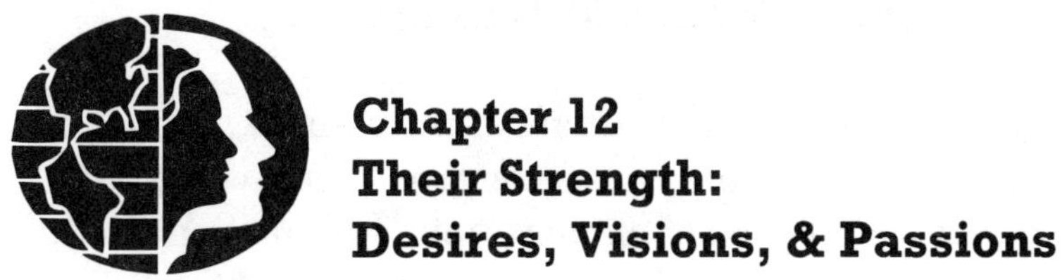

Chapter 12
Their Strength: Desires, Visions, & Passions

Many people live with weak desires, little vision, and no passion. They never will be Kings.

Kings yield to the drive within their hearts. They are not afraid of it. They realize that strength comes from desires and passion God put in their hearts. They embrace that strength. They understand that faith comes from the throne of the heart—which is also the seat of desires.

Desires give birth to vision. Vision empowers life. In contrast,

> *Where there is no vision, the people perish....*
> (Prov. 29:18 KJV)

Leaders know this. Kings need this. You must embrace it.

Passion energizes vision. Without fuel the motor will not run. Without fire the wood never will burn. Without passion you are just a slave plodding through life waiting for retirement. You need more!

In reality, you never will release that fire within unless you believe that God wants you to do so. If your mind is filled with a sin-consciousness, then you will doubt every bit of energy within yourself. If your theology tells you to be a slave, then you will spend your days waiting for someone else to give you orders.

Of course, the person who lives without dreams

may appear humble, unassuming, meek, and even holy, but it is time you recognize it for what it is—bondage. Come out of slavery now. Reign with God!

God Is Working in You

In the Old Testament we see God dealing with people by giving His commandments. In response, many tried to live as obedient slaves, trying to bring every action into submission to the list of "Do's and Don'ts." But we who live on this side of the New Testament have a clearer revelation of how God wants to work in our lives. God is in us. We are His Temple. We are His hands and feet.

> *...for it is God who works in you to will and to act according to his good purpose.*
> (Phil. 2:13)

God is writing His laws on our hearts. He is giving us His desires.

Your desires are not contrary to God's desires. Of course, you may have a few fleshly, carnal thoughts and ideas. But if your heart is to please God, then He is molding your desires to match His. If you are walking with Him, then the vast majority of your desires are already the same as His.

Do you want to know what God wants accomplished in this world? Then ask Christians what they want accomplished. Most will tell you that they want blessings for their families, young people excited about God, a church that loves, cares, and nurtures the presence of God, prosperity for their communities, a safe and wholesome environment, and peace throughout the world. God's desires are not different from your desires. Think about it.

God longs to pour out His heart and make His thoughts known to us (I Cor. 1:10-12). God is looking for relationships in which we share our thoughts with Him and He shares His thoughts with us. We were created for such communion and companionship.

Compare it with marriage. A man and woman in love become one in heart and mind. Their desires and plans merge. They understand one another. As they talk, they often can finish each other's sentences. They become one.

This is how Paul explains our relationship with God.

> *But he who unites himself with the Lord*
> *is one with Him in spirit.* (I Cor. 6:17)

The Spirit moving through you is God's Spirit.

As children, we used to purchase from the local candy store straws filled with sweet-flavored powder. If we sucked water through the straw, it would come out tasting delightful. In similar fashion, God's Spirit flows through the Christian's heart. It picks up some flavor. Your flavor. My flavor. When the Spirit flows through me, it manifests as all the fruit in my life. When the Spirit flows through you, it may manifest as a businessperson, an entrepreneur, a congressman, a teacher, a banker, a parent, an athlete, an entertainer, an artist, or any other form which brings your gifts and talents into the Earth.

This is the reason you can pursue your dreams, follow your desires, trust your heart, and know that God will steer you into the center of His blessings and perfect will.

Live in Resurrection Life

Of course, you may have a few carnal desires. Of course, you struggle with some fleshly thoughts. But that is no reason to sever the source of life within you.

Too many Christians live on the other side of the cross. By this I mean they see themselves hanging on the cross with Jesus. They are obsessed with ideas about crucifying themselves—dying to their own thoughts and desires. They envision themselves in the Garden of Gethsemane crying out to God saying, "Not my will, but Thy will be done!"

Christian maturity does go through a death and resurrection where we learn to put Jesus first (Matt 6:33) We just can't camp in the tomb. I have good news for you: Once you learn "brokenness" your will is God's will. Your passion reflects His heart.

Furthermore, Jesus has risen from the dead and He ascended into Heaven. You have been raised to be seated with Him in heavenly places (Eph. 2:4-6). He died so you don't have to. He lives so now you can live.

Of course, there will be a few carnal desires which will need to be put to death from time to time. Of course, you may be tested at some point of your life as Jesus was in the Garden of Gethsemane. But don't live in that Garden of Weeping. Live on this side of the cross. Live in the resurrection and ascension.

Jesus is in you. He lives there in your heart. He really does. He is not against you. He wants you to succeed:

> *May he give you* ***the desire of your heart*** *and make all* ***your plans*** *succeed.*
> (Ps. 20:4) [Emp. Added]

Your desires! Your plans! Succeed!

When Your Passions Reflect God's Heart

Kings function as sons of God. Sons have passion for their Father's business. Passion begins when they find their hearts' desires and begin to implement them.

I am talking about a passion for your career. For getting out of bed in the morning. For planning long range. For wise investments. For marketing strategies. For innovations and new ideas. For dialogue and relationship building. For competition and integrity. For sales and success! For influencing the community in which you live.

You have a calling. It is built into your personality, your gifts, and the desires of your heart. God put it there. Until you activate the real desires of your heart, you never will be fully passionate about God or anything you do for Him. You'll just be a servant going through the motions looking for a wage, a retirement, and an eternal pension. There's more to life than that! It is people living out the desires of their hearts with a contagious sense of adventure, passion, and fruit.

Consider the words of John Elridge, the author of the best-selling Christian book, *Wild at Heart:*

> Don't ask what the world needs. Ask what makes you fully alive, because the world needs you fully alive.

Meditate on this. It will set you free.

Of course, I'm not teaching unbridled enthusiasm. We need to check ourselves from time to time. We need to reign in our excesses. We need to stay in right relationships which keep our lives on course. We must not give ourselves to passions which overrun the welfare of our neighbors. No, I am not teaching unbridled enthusiasm, but **I am teaching enthusiasm**.

Passion is your friend. It is God-given. He put it in your nature.

Passion Leads to Holiness

Does God really want you to live this way? Let me boldly declare to you that this is the only path to holiness.

Traditionally, holiness is defined as the absence of sin, which really is more a byproduct of holiness. Real holiness springs out of the passion and fruit that go with the positive things we naturally and passionately desire to do; things that match the heart of God.

This means that to attain holiness, we cannot focus solely on sin and be successful. In a sin-oriented theology, we force ourselves into a discipline of religious obedience, integrity, perseverance in trials, faithfulness, serving in another person's vision, learning authority and submission—all things we can try to generate in our own strength without God.

This is the slave/servant approach to God. It is fueled by the theology that we are totally depraved and must superimpose God's desires over our own evil desires. Because of this mentality, we fear we're always one step away from succumbing to the temptation, to "do our own thing."

I want you to do your own thing—because your thing is God's thing! Too extreme? God created you with desires and passions we need to pursue in His way. But, they must be pursued. They reflect His heart. You are an expression of God's heart

Of course, all people sin, and we need Jesus Christ in our lives as Savior. At times we may fear that carnal appetites will take over and we could get far from God. But for the most part, the opposite is true. Once a person connects with his/her destiny, he/she will do whatever is necessary to correct his/her own sin to get to the end goal. When people actually come to believe that God is with them and in them, they become sensitive to the Holy Spirit Who leads them to even greater sanctification.

Just Do It

Once we dare accept the truth that God is with

us, we release incredible energy into and through our own lives. When we connect with our birthright, we activate our own destiny and lock onto the future.

If you want to be a King, think like a King. Act like a King. Apply the words of King Solomon:

> *...follow the impulses of your heart and the desires of your eyes. Yet know that God will bring you to judgment for all these things.* (Eccl. 11:9 NASV)

The impulses of your heart. The desires of your eyes. Follow them. Yield. Be passionate! Of course, God will hold you accountable, so stay in tune with Him. But while you do, go for it! Light the fire!

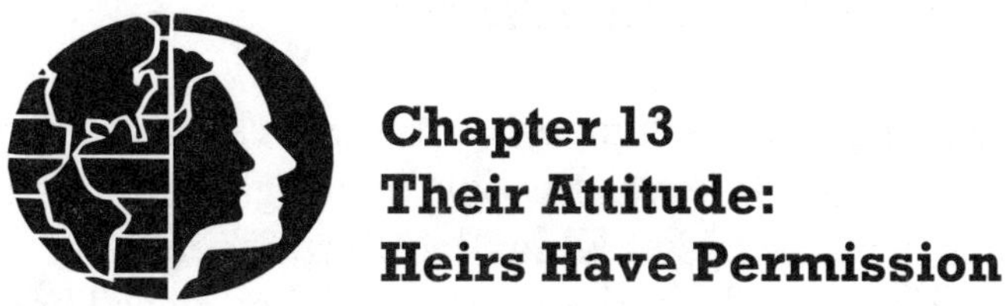

Chapter 13
Their Attitude: Heirs Have Permission

Kings are people who have healthy self-concepts. They sense permission from God to be bold, creative, competitive, decisive, and willing to take risks.

Where do these qualities originate? From God. We are created in His image.

Furthermore, Christians have rights.

> *But as many as received Him, to those He gave the right to become children of God, even to those who believe in His name....*
> (John 1:12)

You and I have family rights. We have a birthright!

Claiming Your Birthright

As God's representatives on this Earth, we need to establish the will of our Father here. He has placed within each one of us talents, gifts, and abilities to manage some area of life. He is breathing within our hearts, stirring desires, and bringing passions to life according to His purposes.

We need to step out. We each need to claim the land He's given us. We are called to manage this Earth, to bring a portion of this planet under our authority, and in so doing it, establish the will of God. This is the family business.

In stepping out we move from slaves/servants to Sons/Kings. Slaves/servants operate against their own hearts' desires. Sons/Kings look into their hearts for the desires God has placed there. They act. They take dominion. They reign with Christ.

Don't Sell Your Birthright

> *Once when Jacob was cooking some stew, Esau came in from the open country, famished. He said to Jacob, "Quick, let me have some of that red stew! I'm famished!"...Jacob replied, "First sell me your birthright." "Look, I am about to die," Esau said. "What good is the birthright to me?" But Jacob said, "Swear to me first." So he swore an oath to him, selling his birthright to Jacob. Then Jacob gave Esau some bread and some lentil stew. He ate and drank, and then got up and left. So Esau despised his birthright.* (Gen. 25:29-34)

Jacob was a sneaky guy. He probably would not have passed our standards for integrity. However, he had a passion to pursue his desires and he pursued his birthright. God likes that kind of passion so much that He focused His love on Jacob, in spite of his character flaws.

> *Just as it is written: "Jacob I loved, but Esau I hated."* (Rom. 9:13)

Living at the level of fulfilling our hearts' desires is our birthright as Christians. We can live as sons rather than slaves. The enemy would love for us to sell that right. Don't. Don't give away what God has put in your heart. God likes people who pursue their visions.

Trust God

What if you pursued the desire of your heart and it really was not God's desire? Don't worry, be happy. We still can trust God to intervene in several ways:

1. Our wrong desires come to nothing without God's blessing on them (John 15:5).
2. God loves us enough to discipline us as His wayward kids (Heb. 12:4-6).
3. When we make a mistake, He doesn't cut us off in our relationships with Him. He continues to speak to us and gives opportunities to respond. He still reveals His heart to us and leads us in His will (Prov. 1:23).

All of us have made mistakes regarding our hearts' desires. Many also have made a vow, "I'm never going to step out again and trust my heart's desire because I've gotten burned." What this vow really says is this: "I'm never again going to trust God or the intuitive vision He has placed within me."

This vow does several things that eventually have to be reversed. First, it puts us back into the camp of servants, living under no vision or the vision of another person. Second, the vow pushes us toward believing in a distant, all-controlling God with Whom it is difficult to relate. Third, this vow puts us out of touch with our hearts. Then we even have difficulty getting in touch with our desires or the desires of God's heart.

Those vows have to be reversed. We have to forgive ourselves and others. If in the turmoil of not seeing goals met we became angry at God, we must be reconciled to Him. Once healed of past hurts, we can choose to set our hearts on the vision God has for us. Just as we can set our hearts on carnal things, we also can choose to set our hearts on all the benefits of the plan of God—it's a much better choice from every angle!

Few of us realize how much freedom (or permission) we really have within the will of God. He's very willing to show us His plans to build the Kingdom. He's also willing to engage us in a prayer conversation about what part we are to play. His will is going to prevail in the Earth. He does have a destiny for us, but how we fulfill it is determined with our participation. We choose to be players, and we choose to engage the desires of our hearts and find the synergy between our desires and God's desires.

That freedom allows for mistakes.

Most of us would be more comfortable with a God who made all the decisions. God, however, isn't looking for robots. He wants relationships with people who are willing to take responsibility for His business. He wants Kings to rule with Him.

Chapter 14
Their Prayer: Asking Whatsoever

Kings operate as friends of God and they pray out of the desires of their hearts.

Solomon is a good example of how God deals with Kings in prayer. First, Solomon served God out of love and understood the importance of the kingly heritage that came down to him from his father, David:

> *Solomon showed his love for the LORD by walking according to the statutes of his father David....* (I Kings 3:2-3)

The real desire of Solomon's heart was to do a good job of leading God's people. It's important to realize that Kings may have vast resources, influence, and wealth, but they view those things as tools to obtain the desires of their hearts and of God's heart. Notice how God deals with Solomon's kingly mentality:

> *At Gibeon the LORD appeared to Solomon during the night in a dream, and God said, "**Ask for whatever you want me to give you.**"*
> (I Kings 3:5) [Emp. added]

Solomon asked for the wisdom and ability to govern Israel (his heart's desire). He postured himself as a servant before God in verse 8. Now notice God's response:

> *The Lord was pleased that Solomon had asked for this. So God said to him, "Since you have asked for this and not for long life or wealth for yourself, nor have asked for the death of your enemies but for discernment in administering justice, I will do what you have asked. I will give you a wise and discerning heart, so that there will never have been anyone like you, nor will there ever be. Moreover, I will give you what you have not asked for—both riches and honor—so that in your lifetime you will have no equal among Kings...."* (I Kings 3:10-13)

God gave Solomon his request and added riches, honor, and long life—these were not just presents from God, but the resources that were necessary for Solomon to complete his destiny in the Kingdom.

Instead of thinking of God's invitation to Solomon as unique, I want you to see it as a general invitation to Kings that can be found throughout the Bible.

> *"If you remain in me and my words remain in you,* ***ask whatever you wish, and it will be given you****. This is to my Father's glory, that you bear much fruit, showing yourselves to be my disciples."*
> (John 15:6-8) [Emp. added]

> *So Jesus answered and said to them, "Have faith in God. For assuredly, I say to you, whoever says to this mountain, 'Be removed and be cast into the sea,' and does not doubt in his heart, but believes that those things he says will be done,* ***he will have whatever he says****. Therefore I say to you, whatever things you ask when you pray, believe that you receive them, and you will have them."*
> (Mark 11:22-24 NKJV) [Emp. Added]

> *"Until now you have not asked for anything in my name.* ***Ask and you will receive****, and your joy will be complete."*
> (John 16:24) [Emp added]

See? God's offer to Solomon applies to you as well! Are you willing to ask God for "whatever you wish"? The key to answered prayer for Kings resides in the desires of their hearts. God is looking for people who share His heart to expand the Kingdom. When God finds those people, He grants the desires of their hearts.

> *"Ask and it will be given to you; seek and you will find; knock and the door will be opened to you. For everyone who asks receives; he who seeks finds; and to him who knocks, the door will be opened."*
> (Matt. 7:7-8)

"Again, I tell you that if two of you on earth agree about anything you ask for, it will be done for you by my Father in heaven. For where two or three come together in my name, there am I with them." (Matt. 18:19-20)

"'If you can?'" said Jesus. "Everything is possible for him who believes." (Mark 9:23)

"Therefore I tell you, whatever you ask for in prayer, believe that you have received it, and it will be yours. And when you stand praying, if you hold anything against anyone, forgive him, so that your Father in heaven may forgive you your sins." (Mark 11:24-25)

"I tell you the truth, anyone who has faith in me will do what I have been doing. He will do even greater things than these, because I am going to the Father. And I will do whatever you ask in my name, so that the Son may bring glory to the Father. You may ask me for anything in my name, and I will do it." (John 14:11-14)

"If you abide in Me, and My words abide in you, you will ask what you desire, and it shall be done for you. By this My

> *Father is glorified, that you bear much fruit; so you will be My disciples."*
> (John 15:7-8 NKJV)

> *Dear friends, if our hearts do not condemn us, we have confidence before God and receive from him anything we ask, because we obey his commands and do what pleases him.* (I John 3:21-22)

> *This is the confidence we have in approaching God: that if we ask anything according to his will, he hears us. And if we know that he hears us—whatever we ask—we know that we have what we asked of him.* (I John 5:14-15)

What if it is true? What if God really will answer your prayers? What if He really is your business partner? What does this mean for your business, your home, your family?

> *"I tell you the truth, my Father will give you whatever you ask in my name. Until now you have not asked for anything in my name. Ask and you will receive, and your joy will be complete."*
> (John 16:23-24)

We are not alone. Our Father is a friend. He wants to stay involved. He wants to help us.

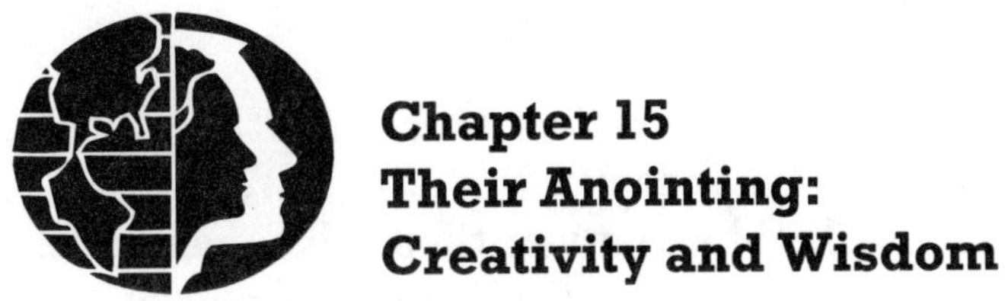

Chapter 15
Their Anointing: Creativity and Wisdom

Kings are people who think creatively, as God does. The inquisitive spirit is the childlike heart that Jesus encouraged. Kings employ this outlook in every venture they undertake, from arts to business to politics to technology.

Solomon said it best in Proverbs.

> *It is the glory of God to conceal a matter; to search out a matter is the glory of Kings.* (Prov. 25:2)

Creative breakthrough is a core motivation for Kings and it comes in many forms:

- A businessman discovers a new product for a new market and quadruples his profit.
- A poet finds the perfect end to his verse with rhyme, meter, and stunning imagery.
- A scientist invents a new process that greatly simplifies a manufacturing procedure.
- A musician finds the perfect hook line for his lyric.
- A teacher discovers a key to motivate a problem child and frees the entire class.
- A congressman articulates a compromise that unites opposing viewpoints.
- A married person finds the key to open his/her spouse's heart in deep communication.

The breakthroughs reflect kingly attitudes. Kings believe there is an answer and they are willing to search for it. They have given themselves permission to "create" just as God does. The humble obedience of slaves and servants never approaches the throne of such a rich experience. Great Kings know how to let God work through their minds and hearts. They are God's "mighty men" that do exploits.

Gifted As King Solomon

Solomon was a King who did just that. Here's his request:

> *"So give your servant a discerning heart to govern your people and to distinguish between right and wrong. For who is able to govern this great people of yours?" The Lord was pleased that Solomon had asked for this.* (I Kings 3:8-10)

And here's the result:

> *God gave Solomon wisdom and very great insight, and a breadth of understanding as measureless as the sand on the seashore.* (I Kings 4:29)

He was a great King with a great servant's heart. His leadership blessed the people he served and the God he served. Kings are not afraid of authority. They use their wealth and influence to bless nations.

Dream With God

Creativity is more than a natural process. As Paul wrote, "For who among men knows the thoughts of a man except the man's spirit within him?" (I Cor. 2:11). The spirit within reaches for answers. It enlightens the mind as a flashlight shining on the screen of the mind. Answers come. Innovations formulate. Missing pieces fit into the puzzle.

Yet we are not alone in this creative process. Paul went on to explain how God reveals to us mysteries by His Spirit (I Cor. 2:9-12). The breath of God merges with the spirit of a person and creativity is the result. Spirit touches spirit. Ideas are conceived. Answers are born.

Jesus encouraged His followers to "Look at the birds of the air...see how the lilies of the field grow" (Matt 6:26-28). When we put ourselves in such a state of mind where anxieties are set aside, then life flows from God as light flows from the sun. Creative energy bathes our souls. When we anchor ourselves in the heart of God, His heart pumps life fluids into our beings. We come alive. We become creative.

This will work for you. As you set aside your anxieties about food, clothing, and business, then look to your Father, "...all these things shall be added unto you" (Matt. 6:33 KJV). He cares for the lilies of the field, so certainly He will care for you. Touch His heart and He will kiss you with the breath of His nature.

The insolvable is solved. The path is cleared. The door is opened. All things are possible to "believers".

Think As a King

I recently read a great biography entitled, *R. G. LeTourneau: Mover of Men and Mountains.* LeTourneau was a King in every sense of the word. Buried in the back of the book is a little story of how he accepted more construction contracts than he could fulfill. His choices were to try to get out of the contracts, to buy existing machinery to do the jobs faster, or expand his own factory and build more machines himself. His God-inspired creativity carried him through this crisis. Instead of building or buying conventional machines, he invented and built larger machines to do the work in less time. The result was that although he was overextended badly, he delivered on all his contracts on schedule. More importantly, he positioned himself ahead of his competition because of his innovations.

Kings have an ability to look at intimidating problems and find innovative answers. They know intuitively and theologically that no problem is too big for God. And they usually have a track record for defeating giants.

Chapter 16
Their Mindset: Abundance Is God's Will

Too many Christians have a limited view of finances and resources. They tithe, their needs are met, and the bills get paid, but that's about it. They see that they are getting by, so they leave well enough alone. It translates into the following life story.

John Doe was encouraged to get a college education. So at 18, after graduating from high school and moving out of the house, he bought a car and spent four years in college. His parents paid for part of his education, and he took out a loan to pay for the rest. Between the car and college loan, he graduated with a debt of $30,000, and then bought a new car for $25,000 (total debt = $55,000). He found his sweetheart in college and got married within a year of graduation. Next came that first small but cozy house for an additional $120,000 of debt, bringing the total to $175,000. Someone told him his home mortgage debt was really equity, so he doesn't count it as debt—however, he pays $10,000 a year in interest. His job was good enough to buy his wife a second car and start a family. He heard that children cost $200,000 each to raise, but didn't believe it or plan for it.

At age 35, the kids were four, six, and eight, and the new car was a minivan. At 45, John's oldest started college and his wife went back to work in the marketplace. His debt was over $200,000 since progress on paying it off was offset by upgrading the house, buying new cars, and adding the boat. He then started paying the bills for college. He and his wife's income put them in too high a salary bracket for the kids to qualify for grants or scholarships, so he paid the $12,000 per year, per child, which consumed slightly more than his wife's salary until the kids graduated.

They are now 55. They may or may not get the house paid off before they retire to live on a pension and social security. The bottom line is that they lived from paycheck to paycheck for 30 years without a moment of excess. When they die, the estate will be rounded off to zero, and the children will carry the same poverty mentality into the next generation. We call this the great American lifestyle.

That story sounds so familiar, it's painful. It's a lifestyle that has no expectation that God could intervene with the "ability to produce wealth," as He promised:

> *But remember the LORD your God, for it is he who gives you the ability to produce wealth, and so confirms his covenant, which he swore to your forefathers, as it is today.* (Deut. 8:17-18)

Putting the issue in simple terms, Kings cannot be content to live the typical, month-to-month, barely-get-by lifestyle. For Kings, it represents a poverty mentality that denies the abundance that God has for them—the very abundance that they require to carry out God's business. For all Christians, and especially Kings, the strongholds that keep them from receiving God's abundance must be removed. As the Scripture says:

> *For though we live in the world, we do not wage war as the world does. The weapons we fight with are not the weapons of the world. On the contrary, they have divine power to demolish strongholds. We demolish arguments and every pretension that sets itself up against the knowledge of God, and we take captive every thought to make it obedient to Christ.* (II Cor. 10:3-5)

Kings express the characteristics of God in important ways: His generosity, His abundance, and the increase of His Kingdom. That emphasis is not the same for priestly and prophetic ministries. They carry different, but equally important, aspects of God. When we read promises of financial prosperity, such as those below, we should understand that they pertain especially to Kings, whose ministries require such promises.

Kings not only believe for financial prosperity, they embrace the conditions that make these promises a reality. Each of the following verses have both conditions and promises. *Kings read both.*

> *So if you faithfully obey the commands I*

> *am giving you today—to love the LORD your God and to serve him with all your heart and with all your soul—then I will send rain on your land in its season, both autumn and spring rains, so that you may gather in your grain, new wine and oil. I will provide grass in the fields for your cattle, and you will eat and be satisfied.* (Deut. 11:13-15)

> *Give generously to him and do so without a grudging heart; then because of this the LORD your God will bless you in all your work and in everything you put your hand to....*
> (Deut. 15:10-11; see also 14:28-29)

> *The blessing of the LORD brings wealth, and he adds no trouble to it.*
> (Prov. 10:22)

> *"Will a man rob God? Yet you rob me. But you ask, 'How do we rob you?' In tithes and offerings. You are under a curse—the whole nation of you—because you are robbing me. Bring the whole tithe into the storehouse, that there may be food in my house. Test me in this," says the LORD Almighty, "and see if I will not throw open the floodgates of heaven and pour out so much blessing that you will not have room enough for it. I will*

prevent pests from devouring your crops, and the vines in your fields will not cast their fruit," says the LORD Almighty.
(Mal. 3:8-12)

But seek first his kingdom and his righteousness, and all these things will be given to you as well. (Matt. 6:33)

And everyone who has left houses or brothers or sisters or father or mother or children or fields for my sake will receive a hundred times as much and will inherit eternal life. (Matt. 19:29)

"Give, and it will be given to you. A good measure, pressed down, shaken together and running over, will be poured into your lap. For with the measure you use, it will be measured to you." (Luke 6:38)

Holding these promises for abundance, the King advances with confidence.

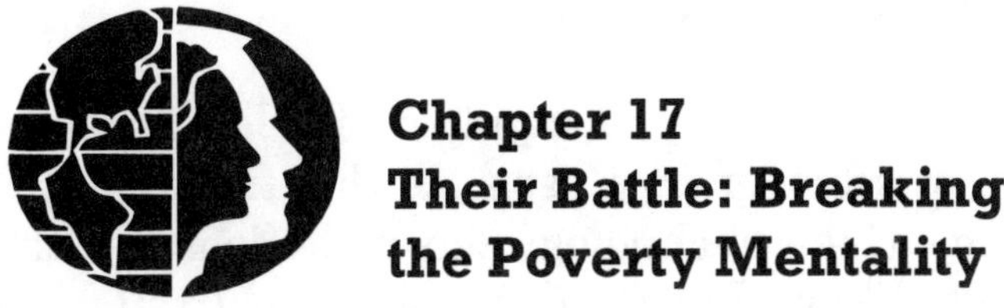

Chapter 17
Their Battle: Breaking the Poverty Mentality

For a King to succeed, he must break strongholds. Here are six strongholds (lies) that must be broken to release Kings into their God-given inheritances.

Lie # 1: The Resource Pie Is a Fixed Quantity

This erroneous economic theory implies that a larger slice of the resource pie for you means a smaller slice for me. The concept of supply and demand assumes that there is a finite supply of a commodity and that demand governs both its price and the rate at which the supply will be exhausted. An example of this is oil. Our economy routinely experiences various swings of confidence in our oil supply. These swings are based on the fear that if oil supplies were exhausted, our whole standard of living would take a big step back toward the Stone Age! Since we believe that the resource pie is fixed—that the supply of oil is finite—we've made the Middle-Eastern nations that sit on the world's oil supply incredibly wealthy.

What we fail to realize is that although the supply of oil is finite, the supply of energy—what oil truly is to our economy—is anything but fixed. Economies historically have corrected themselves when the supply and demand drove a commodity out of existence. Several centuries back, the civilized world relied on whale blubber to supply oil for lamps and a multitude of other energy uses. As this finite supply diminished, a new technology dawned. Consider the words of Paul Zane Pilzer in his book *God Wants You to be Rich*:

> The world's first major energy crisis struck in the middle of the nineteenth century, when the worldwide supply of whales dwindled, mostly as a result of the Yankee efficiency in harvesting them. In 1859, over ten thousand whales were harvested from the North Atlantic alone; this caused a worldwide shortage in whale products on both sides of the ocean.
>
> But in 1859, just as the doomsayers were predicting the end of their economies, due to the shortage of whale products, another burst of Yankee ingenuity came onto the scene with a lower-cost substitute for virtually all whale-based products. Col. Edwin L. Drake drilled the world's first successful oil well in Titusville, Pennsylvania, on August 27, 1859, ushering in the modern petroleum age.

In a similar vein, coal was a major energy resource for domestic and industrial power, including railroad power, until 1950 when supplies gradually diminished. Again, our economy moved on to other supplies of energy. Throughout history, when a resource became exhausted, a different (and usually better) resource always has been found.

God did not have failure in mind when He created the universe. We are not going to run out of something we truly need—in this case, energy. In every crisis, God will use the ingenuity of Kings to find the needed resources. Although we are currently an oil-based economy, the day will come when technology will open a new source of energy. Before the drought even starts, God sends His Josephs to prepare for the needs of His family.

We serve a God of abundance. Creativity united with faith opens our eyes to see Him and His answers.

Lie # 2: It Is Spiritual to Be Poor

The cousin of "the resource pie is fixed," is another form of the poverty mentality that holds poverty as an esteemed spiritual quality. Related to this, Christians often judge abundance to be excessive materialism.

Most people think of Mother Theresa as the epitome of humility and generosity. And this is true—she really was humble and generous. She also had access to her own air transportation, a support staff, and made million-dollar decisions. She was a King in disguise! Mother Teresa outwardly disavowed power, fame, and wealth, and yet she became powerful, famous, and generated enough wealth to support a worldwide organization with 4,000 employees. Her ministry targeted the poor outside the Church, and she expanded the Kingdom of God by reaching out to them. But to say she shared a life of poverty denies the reality of the resources that flowed to and through her.

Lie # 3: The Wealthy Are Arrogant

Too often we've looked at Kings with their wealth and assumed they were proud, unapproachable, and consumed with selfish materialism. We need to rethink this stereotype of the wealthy.

The reason they have wealth in the first place is usually because they already are tapped into a spiritual principle...at a deeper level than some of their poor but pious critics! *God promotes humility.*

> *God opposes the proud, but gives grace to the humble.* (James 4:6)

> *...humility comes before honor.* (Prov. 15:33)

> *Before his downfall a man's heart is proud, but humility comes before honor.* (Prov. 18:12)

> *Humility and the fear of the LORD bring wealth and honor and life.* (Prov. 22:4)

> *He mocks proud mockers but gives grace to the humble.* (Prov. 3:34)

Lie # 4: God Automatically Will Transfer Wealth in the Last Days

This is a belief which some Christians hold that God will transfer wealth from the heathens to Christians before Jesus' return. Some of the verses used to support this belief are listed below. This emphasis is unbalanced, however, because it focuses a negative faith toward the lost instead of a positive belief in the real source—God.

> *A good man leaves an inheritance for his children's children, but a sinner's wealth is stored up for the righteous.*
>
> (Prov. 13:22)

> *He who increases his wealth by exorbitant interest amasses it for another, who will be kind to the poor.*
>
> (Prov. 28:8)

> *To the man who pleases him, God gives wisdom, knowledge and happiness, but to the sinner he gives the task of gathering and storing up wealth to hand it over to the one who pleases God....*
>
> (Eccl. 2:26)

In certain Christian circles, the transfer of wealth is preached in a way that directs the faith of its adherents to envy, and at some levels, to curse non-Christians. The real heart of God is to reach the lost, regardless of their financial status. The heart of God is best seen in His promise to Abraham.

> *"I will make you into a great nation and I will bless you; I will make your name great, and you will be a blessing. I will bless those who bless you, and whoever curses you I will curse; and all peoples on earth will be blessed through you."*
>
> (Gen. 12:2-3)

Great wealth is coming to the Kingdom of God through Kings, but it will not be at the expense of others. It will be for the blessing of others. All peoples on Earth will be blessed through Kings such as you.

Instead of transferring wealth from heathens to Christians, God is transferring blessings from Christians to every nation, tongue, tribe, and people. That's the essence of the Great Commission. We're here to export good news. We're not here to announce to the world that their wealth is flowing out of their pockets and into ours. That kind of message does not make converts. Kings are examples of Christians that have wealth, leadership, and influence. And, these use those attributes to make others successful. Kings are "servants" with some really good news and the ability to make the good news a reality for others.

> *And then he told them, "You are to go into all the world and preach the Good News to everyone, everywhere."*
>
> (Mark 16:15 TLB)

Lie # 5: Businesspeople Are Not as Spiritual as People in Full-time Ministry

Jesus was no less spiritual while He was a carpenter than when He launched His three-year ministry.

Kings operating in the secular world are no less spiritual than biblical examples of Kings such as Abraham, David, and Paul. This particular stronghold will crack when Kings begin to show themselves in the mission of expanding the Kingdom.

Lie # 6: Priests Have the Vision, While Kings Have the Provision

This stronghold presumes that marketplace ministries have no more use than to bring finances into the Church to expand its ministries under the direction of the pastor (a Priest). The fallacy is that Priests didn't have the vision for the exploits of Kings, as I have discussed throughout this book. A Priest's focus is in the Temple; a King's focus is expanding God's Kingdom to fill the Earth.

I do believe many great examples of Kings and Priests working together exist in the large churches. Nearly every large church has a pastor who has inspired Kings to work with him and see the vision of the local church come to pass. I wholeheartedly endorse such teamwork. My only reservation is that the call on Kings is far bigger than funding the church building program. Kings are God's instrument to expand the Kingdom outside the church. We must build strong churches with dynamic pastors. But to reach the nations, we've got to start turning our cities upside down. This will be costly and time consuming. It goes far beyond the scope of what any local pastor or group of pastors could support. It will take pastors, Prophets and Kings working together....acknowledging and respecting the differences in their roles.

When Kings Break Poverty

Imagine what God could do through us if we had greater resources. Kings are the answer to those greater resources. I'll use an example from my own life.

In 1990, my wife and I felt led to start a church. Several other families expressed an interest, and we eventually rented a motel ballroom on Sunday's and launched Columbia Christian Fellowship. It was exciting, it grew, we moved into a permanent facility and, after ten years, it had a very happy ending. We were able to turn over a congregation to a new pastor who was raised from within our own church. We gave him the building with six payments left. The church could seat about 150-200 and it had a full basement with a kitchen. It also had a separate office building, a separate childcare facility, and extra space for parking.

Sounds easy doesn't it? Well, it wasn't. We first spent five years in that motel. Every service required starting an hour early to haul all the music equipment (speakers, electric piano, sound board, drums, guitars, etc.). I hauled them back and forth from my home for three years before we built a portable container that we kept at the motel. Church members graciously helped us with the details so the work load was shared, but in hindsight, we were missing the real influence of Kings. We did it the hard way.

In our second church plant, we started over again in a motel. This time I was clever enough to have the worship leader haul the equipment back and forth! The whole process changed, though, when a prophetic person in our church found an available building and a King put an extra $10,000 in the offering so we could remodel and move in—otherwise we would have continued, stuck in our motel. This second time around was made so much easier by the ministry of a King.

Kings have an ability to find the next step of growth and the resources required to go with it.

Conclusion to Part III

When kingly sons accept responsibility for the family business, abundance and prosperity begin to flow and the poverty mindset has to flee. The blessing of God is for all areas of life.

- We all need to hear God's voice and long to be in His presence daily. There is no shortage of His presence or His Word. We can have as much as we want. You can go talk to God. You can dream dreams and see visions that display the revelation of God (Acts 2:17). There is no shortage of God to satisfy your hunger to experience Him.

- We all need to look at the fruit of our lives: To how many people have we witnessed? How many have we led to the Lord? We may see poverty in those areas, but God has abundance for us.

- We need to look at broken relationships in marriages and families. We may see a deficit of love but God is willing that our cup overflow with love in a way that blesses relationships so that the need for love is satisfied to the point of export.

- Most of us don't think of ourselves as creative. Start now! God can work through your creativity and flood you with new and fruitful ideas.

Part IV
The Personal Lives of Kings

In Part II, we saw that Kings stand on the theological foundation of the openness and personhood of God, the nature of humanity (having been created in God's image), and an optimistic view of the future. These platforms are a King's motivation. In Part III we discussed the motivations of Kings in ministry. We endeavored to understand why Kings are bold, creative, competitive, and prosperous. We saw a connection between a personal God sharing His business with Kings and a King's passion and drive.

If we stop here, it will appear that Kings are driven, goal-oriented, type-A personalities with whom it is nearly impossible to live. Indeed, that may be the opinion of some of those who live with Kings. However, I want to present a different picture of Kings. I want to look into their personal lives. Let's examine where Kings live.

Chapter 18
His Love: God

Kings are lovers of God first and workers for God second. They operate out of a relationship with Him.

Question #1 – What's the Priority?

If we could ask King David, "What was your number-one priority?" He probably would answer from a Psalm he wrote:

One thing I have desired of the LORD,
That will I seek:
That I may dwell in the house of the
LORD
All the days of my life,
To behold the beauty of the LORD,
And to inquire in His temple.
(Ps. 27:4 NKJV)

David's highest desire was the Lord Himself. He wanted to be in God's house, see His beauty, and ask Him questions. He was in love with the Lord. To bring this home, turn the clock back to when you first dated your spouse and fell in love. You wanted to go to his/her house, gaze on his/her beauty, and talk for hours. Love causes us to do those things. The Lord wants us to fall in love with Him the same way. In fact, Jesus cited as the first and most important commandment: loving God with all one's heart, soul, mind, and strength.

Kings are "serving lovers" not "loving servants." The term "loving servant" is really an oxymoron because you really can't serve those you don't love—whether it's God or people! People who force themselves to do what they really don't want to do, never can put their hearts into it and are seldom successful. On the other hand, people in love always find a way to express that love. You can "serve" those you don't love, but it has the same dedicational pull as slavery.

Question #2 – Why Love God?

Okay, David, we know that loving God is your first priority. Now tell us why. What's the real reason you put "loving God" as the first order of business? What's your definition of the secret of life?

David likely would reply that he was motivated by the pleasures of God. Does it sound like carnal desires? It's not. David found something in God that delighted Him as nothing else in this world.

You will show me the path of life;
In Your presence is fullness of joy;
At Your right hand are pleasures
forevermore. (Ps. 16:11 NKJV)

How priceless is your unfailing love!
Both high and low among men find
refuge in the shadow of your wings.

They feast on the abundance of your
house; you give them drink from
your river of delights.
For with you is the fountain of life;
in your light we see light.
(Ps. 36:7-9)

When David was with God, he found joy and pleasure. He described the experience as drinking from God's river of delights. Get the picture? David had fun when he was with God! He enjoyed God and God enjoyed him.

Nothing David did as King brought more joy to him than his personal experience with God. His motivation didn't come from his great exploits or his great wealth; those were all a distant second to his relationship with God

Question #3 – What about Me?

God is graduating servants to lovers. Kings have big destinies—so big that if we fully understood the work involved, we probably would pass (or pass out). Things such as starting businesses require a huge amount of energy. It has to be a labor of love. The only motivation that can carry us entirely through to the fullness of our calling is the sheer joy of walking with God. Servants and slaves won't be motivated to stay with God for a lifetime. It's the incredible drawing power of His presence that will carry Kings through to their destinies.

As Mike Bickle wrote in his book, *The Pleasures*

of Loving God:

> Many Christians who reach out to others burn out quickly because they launch out into ministry before they establish in themselves the foundations of being lovers of God. Discouragement, despair, boredom, and frustration will inevitably occur if we do not recognize that we are first called to be lovers. Yes, God has called us to be workers. Yes, we are called to be servants. Yes, we are called to bear the inconveniences of being caregivers to other people. But we must remember that such works of service are a part of the second commandment; they are an overflow of the first commandment.

God is not looking for robots to carry out His plans mindlessly. He's looking for those who will be bonded to Him in love.

> *"In that day," declares the LORD, "you will call me 'my husband'; you will no longer call me 'my master.' "* (Hos. 2:16)

Chapter 19
His Freedom: Live as a Son

Religious traditions keep people enslaved. Jesus sets them free. Yet many people choose to remain in prison. Their voluntary enslavement typically appears in ways that hide or pervert their real identity and personality in Christ.

1. St. Volcano: Slaves/servants try to perform and pray according to the will of God, but since it's never really their wills, they award themselves little vacations from serving God. It plays out similar to the advertising jingle: "You deserve a break today." They work hard at obeying and serving God as best they can, and then reward themselves by escaping from slave-labor for a period. I call them "smoke breaks." Good, church-going people may occasionally get drunk, lose their tempers, watch a dirty movie, or have an affair. In their eyes, they've been working hard for God and that tempting inner voice keeps telling them that they deserve an opportunity to do something they want to do once in a while. It's a playground for the devil. He leads them handcuffed toward destruction.

2. The Preacher: One step beyond the "smoke break servant" is the presumptuous person who believes they understand what God wants and is fully engaged in making it happen (a good thing). It's still not the desire of their own hearts, but they've been modestly successful in serving God out of their intellect instead of the Spirit's leading, and they believe they understand God's agenda. These are the folks who are motivated by guilt—"shame on me." These are also the folks who motivate others with guilt—"shame on you." The preaching equivalent of this level of maturity is all too familiar. Even if we don't have pulpits, we get preachy and try to shame people into performing for God. These folks are real finger pointers. They still take "smoke breaks" but their failures are hidden from others so they don't count against their public image.

3. The Mystic: Some slaves hide behind a cloak of spirituality and do nothing. Many servants resist doing anything in their own strength for fear of being outside of God's will. They still are afraid of their hearts' desires. They purport only to do things in God's strength and God's leading. Typically, these people are the most difficult to work with because they won't lift a finger to help themselves or anyone around them. They tend to be inert, unmotivated, and useless. They have been medicated with religious drugs that leave them lethargic.

Your Unspoken Testimony

> *So you are no longer a slave, but a son.... It is for freedom that Christ has set you free.* (Gal. 4:7-5:1a)

Unsaved people inspect our lives for fruit all the time. They review our lives for dead religious activity and reject us when they find it. They want to know if we're forcing ourselves to do something we really don't enjoy, and *they can tell!* Trust me on this. The world easily can discern whether we're living our lives as servants who secretly detest their master or whether we delight in the Lord to Whom we relate as a friend.

Many unsaved and successful people are very confident in themselves. So much so that they are perfectly comfortable in anyone's company and they easily see into the hearts of others. "Religious" Christians will never have any influence on these successful unbelievers because it is easy for the unbeliever to see that the Christian is not freely living life from their heart. They live life under the bondage of self imposed rules and boundaries; not being true to themselves

Consider the message that you are broadcasting to the world. If you live as a slave, ever-conscious of sins, are you really sharing the Good News? Are your friends happy to hear that they are desperately wicked and that they are incorrigible sinners needing a Savior? Do they see freedom in your life? Do they ever get to see who you really are—with your hair down and mask off? Do they want to live the type of life you are living?

The Good News that our neighbors are hungry to hear is that God is a Father. He is One, "...who satisfies your desires with good things so that your youth is renewed like the eagle's" (Ps. 103:5). Our neighbors need to see that promise living in our lives. They will hear it when we believe it. They will see it when we live it. Be yourself.

Chapter 20
His Play: Remaining Childlike

As we transform from slaves and servants of God to sons, friends, and lovers, we experience freedom to be childlike—to play, to dream, to be intuitive and creative. Children love taking their father's hand and walking with him to places they've never been before. Servants and slaves never expect such attention and wouldn't be comfortable with the experience.

The servant mentality tries to substitute obedience for relationship. This religious mindset tries to please the Lord by offering sacrifices of works they don't enjoy! God has a simple answer for that approach to the throne: He doesn't want it. We have nothing to offer God in terms of sacrificial acts that would please Him.

> *You do not delight in sacrifice, or I would bring it; you do not take pleasure in burnt offerings. The sacrifices of God are a broken spirit; a broken and contrite heart, O God, you will not despise.*
>
> (Ps. 51:16-17)

Servants offer a variety of substitutes for the kind of co-laboring that exists on a "son" level of relationship. Servants feel it's noble to superimpose God's will over their own and do what they really don't want to do. Although that can be a first step in our relationship with God, we can't live there. We have to find the place of delighting in our relationship with God, in our ministry and our vocation. We may mature by progressing through rebellion, to unwilling submission, to willing obedience, and finally to delight. Whatever way we get there, the Lord wants to share the joy of building the Kingdom with us.

> *Sacrifice and offering you did not desire, but my ears you have pierced; burnt offerings and sin offerings you did not require. Then I said, "Here I am, I have come—it is written about me in the scroll. I desire to do your will, O my God; your law is within my heart."*
>
> (Ps. 40:6-8)

Learning to "Delight" in the Lord

Let me introduce you to Bill. He's an avid fisherman and outdoor type who got into a healing ministry after he became a Christian. The Lord has used Bill to pray for people at work, in the healing rooms, and at church during altar calls. Bill doesn't hate fishing now that he's saved. But it is likely that if he had to choose between fishing and healing cancer, he would enjoy the victory over cancer much more. It's a thrill and a delight for Bill to be used by God to see someone healed miraculously. He loves it.

> *The law of God is in his heart; his feet do not slip.* (Ps. 37:31)

I was raised on a ranch and always have enjoyed horses. When I left home, got a job, and got married, it never seemed that we could afford horses. I reasoned that they were something the Lord wanted me to give up. When the kids got to be teenagers, we moved to a home that had enough room for horses. When that happened, I had to adjust my thought process. Now I reasoned that maybe God's will was wide enough that I could dabble in this one hobby, and He would grant me a waiver on His general will. That was nearly ten years ago and here's what I've finally realized. God delights in blessing His kids, and He specifically gave me this outlet. It's smack in the middle of His will for me—it probably always was. The horses are a delight and so is God. I feel free to enjoy those horses fully. Because of this blessing, I feel more in touch with myself, with others, and with God.

Give Yourself Permission to be Childlike

Here's a pathway to spirituality and Christian maturity. Make it your aim to be imaginative, creative, and intuitive—as a child. Here are four steps that will get you started.

1. Laughter – God wants us to learn to laugh again. It will heal your heart and renew your love for God and people.

> *A cheerful heart is good medicine, but a crushed spirit dries up the bones.*
>
> (Prov. 17:22)

2. Ask and Receive – God connects our joy with learning to receive good gifts from Him. Remember the joy of Christmas as a child? Your spiritual life should play out just as unwrapping those gifts. Consider the words of our Lord in John 16:

> *"In that day you will no longer ask [erotao – interrogate] me anything. I tell you the truth, my Father will give you whatever you ask [aiteo] in my name. Until now you have not asked [aieto – place a demand] for anything in my name. Ask [aiteo - place a demand] and you will receive, and your joy will be complete."* (John 16:23-24)
> [Emphasis and Greek words added]

I've inserted the Greek words for "ask" in order to make a point. This verse says we no longer need to interrogate God for things. When we ask, we place a demand (in harmony with what the Father is doing), receive an answer, and our joy is complete. Servants pray without knowing for what to ask, and they don't have any assurance of being heard. Answers are hit and miss at best. The uncertainty is frustrating emotionally and confusing theologically. Servants often protect themselves from failure by ending prayers with the phrase, "...if it be Thy will." Their prayers sound similar to: "Lord, please...we wish You would...if You could just...please make...we hope You will...if it be Thy will." The idea of placing a demand on God's resources is foreign to a servant.

Sons pray from the position of knowing the Father's business. Their prayer is more a confident request premised on the authority of knowing what the Father is doing. Once we know the mind of Christ for a specific situation, we can speak or prophesy the answer into existence. The result is answered prayer, great victories, and great joy. It's thrilling to know the heart of God, pray His will with certainty, and see a miraculous answer. John 16:24 ends with the phrase, "place a demand and you will receive, and your joy will be complete."

3. Pretend – When children pretend, they really just imagine life as they would like to see it. You can be and do anything you want when you pretend—cowboys, doctors, lawyers, firemen, astronauts. If resources didn't constrain you, what would you do to fulfill your perfect dream? What's your pretend scenario? Learn to pay attention to your desires—you'll find God there. Begin to pray, "Father, I give myself permission to dream about the desires you've placed within my heart." Faith begins with pretending.

4. Play – Now, instead of just pretending, begin to confess and act upon your dream. It will feel like play; what you've always wanted to do! If you're going to be the friend of God, you'll have to learn to trust Him to give you the desires of your heart. You have to believe that, "created in His image," means your heart's desires are godly, and that you have authority to speak them into existence, just the way God does.

We're just doing what we see the Father doing. He spoke the desires of His heart into existence and the universe appeared. You should speak your desires into existence, too.

5. Have a Dream – Give yourself permission to dream about your heart's desire and then begin to prophesy it into existence.

> *"'In the last days,' God says, 'I will pour out my Spirit on all people. Your sons and daughters will prophesy, your young men will see visions, your old men will dream dreams. Even on my servants, both men and women, I will pour out my Spirit in those days, and they will prophesy.'"* (Acts 2:17-18)

It's a very simple three-step process:

1. We envision or dream the thing God is putting in our hearts;
2. He pours out His Spirit;
3. We prophesy the dream into existence.

What if it doesn't happen on our schedule? Should we stop dreaming? No! We probably should dream more and give God even more opportunities to speak into our hearts.

I always dreamed about starting a church. For years I thought it was an expression of my carnal appetite for something I shouldn't have. But I was wrong; it was God from the very beginning. As a servant, I hadn't given myself permission to look into the desires of my heart. When I did, I found the will of God. So will you!

Dead religious activity—the kind that depresses God—involves doing what you believe in your mind that God wants you to do, against your own will or desires. A real relationship with God finds God right in the middle of your heart's desires and your mind. Why? Because God created us to both do and to desire His perfect will.

Please don't be afraid of the Holy Spirit's activity in your heart. Give yourself permission to laugh, to pretend, to play, and to live out your dreams. That's where God is.

You can pray this way:

> Lord, we trust that You really did create us as a package of perfect abilities and desires to completely fulfill Your plan for our lives and the desires of our hearts. Thank You Lord, that You've invited us into this level of friendship. It's fun.

Chapter 21
His On-ramp: The Marketplace

When people experience God's presence, they become passionate for Him and passionate for His ministry. The blessing of marketplace ministry is that it provides an on-ramp for ministry on the missionfield of the marketplace. As you read the following testimony, see if you can feel the pain and passion of a King trying to find himself. It expresses the sentiment of millions of Kings who are searching for their ministry on-ramp.

Jim's Testimony

> I'm very much an occupation kind of guy; my job is important to me. It's important that I have something to pour my energy into. This is one reason I like the message I see in your book. It is also the reason I'm willing to fight for it. I feel that I stumbled onto this message (or the meaning of it) years ago as I tried to live two lives: the one that the church structure was telling me I was to live (by that—I mean the Priests in the local body) and the professional life that God was leading me into.
>
> As a supervisor of a small engineering office in South Carolina, I cared for my guys like a pastor cares for his flock. The engineers and designers were my flock. We grew close

and they shared their lives with me. Many confided to me their most intimate life details, and I was able to help. Though I left that assignment four years ago, I'm still close to them in my heart. One died of cancer recently, and I still hurt for missing him. He was mine, and he was taken away.

During my tenure at this office, a conflict developed between the local church I was attending and my job. I was required to pour more and more time and effort into the job—much of it in management issues related to the care of the men and improving the system under which they worked. Because of this, I could not support the church-based ministries, the programs, and the social obligations. I grew apart from those who were pouring their lives into the church. I couldn't relate to them. On Sunday mornings, instead of going to church, I started going to the office and pray. I'd pray for my people, the business, my co-workers, and of course, my loved-ones. Gradually, I saw things less and less like the church did, and grew more involved with the life I felt God was leading me into.

I couldn't understand the schism, but I knew it was real, and it caused a real separation in me. I wondered if I was wrong, if they were wrong, or was I a rogue sheep being separated by the wolf for slaughter? None of those thoughts fit, but still, I had no answer. I felt like I was serving God—REALLY serving

> God—but it didn't make sense compared with the rest of the church. I had no answers.
>
> Until I talked with you and read your manuscript. Then pieces started falling into place. Then it made sense. Then I got excited.
>
> For me, I have to put MPM [Marketplace Ministry] into practice daily, BECAUSE I have no other place to minister. My heart is bursting to minister, but there is no pulpit, no stage, no street corner, not even a skid row mission. I'm called, sent, rooted, and prospering—in the marketplace. And so are most people.
>
> What I call ministry is 99% just living the Christian life. It is rare that I talk to anyone directly about God. Mine is a ministry of living it—the joys and pain, the wrinkles and stains, the highs and lows, the narrow rows.
>
> So yes, this MPM message can reach a lot of people like me, give them hope, give them purpose. It can give them a mission.

As you read Jim's testimony, you can feel his passion for being God's minister in the marketplace. You also can feel his frustration with the church—his calling to minister in the marketplace wasn't recognized or encouraged in his congregation. Here's the good news. Jim will once again find a church home. And, the local church he calls home will be one that recognizes and releases Kings; one that equips them and sends them out into the marketplace. In turn, Jim will bring his friends from the workplace to this oasis of freedom and release....Most of us are Kings.

Ministry in the Church or the Marketplace?

A common mistake is for Kings to feel the passion of a ministry call and assume it only can be expressed in a pulpit through a priestly kind of ministry. As a bi-vocational pastor, I'm well acquainted with what fills the day of full-time pastors and what fills the day of those in the workplace. I'd like to remove the romantic notion of spirituality of which people dream when they envy those in full-time ministry.

The typical pastor spends a lot of time and energy administrating his/her church. They are responsible for programs that deal with various age groups, paying the bills, maintaining facilities, counseling church members, attending meetings, and managing staff. They do pray and preach, but spend much more time dealing with daily problems, conflicts, budgets, and family crises. The bottom line is that full-time ministry isn't going from glory to glory; it's going from mess to mess. Financially your needs are met but your salary comes from the same budget as all those programs that never have enough money. I haven't yet been in a church where there is too much money! The up side of a priestly ministry (pastoring) is that there is a lot of satisfaction in helping people get their lives together. Seeing someone you've spiritually equipped really take off in his/her ministry is a huge blessing. There isn't anything better than seeing your "kids" do well. Pastors take tremendous pride in the accomplishments of their people. Shepherds naturally identify with their sheep. A growing, healthy church has a vibrancy and a presence of God around it that is really exciting.

What if you're called to be a King? It could be a mundane 7:00 AM to 4:30 PM existence that's no fun. It could be a pressure-cooker new business that totally consumes you. It also could be a place where your initiative and creativity can be released to accomplish great things. I believe God is preparing a people to extend revival into our cities. Would you want to be parked in a staff office while others are turning the city upside down for Christ? What if God blessed you financially to the extent that you could serve Him in any capacity you choose? Would you choose that church staff slot or would you choose to...

> *"Heal the sick, cleanse the lepers, raise the dead, cast out devils: freely you have received, freely give."* (Matt. 10:8 KJV)

I say this because after people get saved they realize they have a call on their lives, complete with spiritual gifts and ministry motivations. They see that God already has orchestrated their lives toward doing His will; it is really exciting!...so exciting that we're willing to drop everything and run toward it.

Christians who really get a glimpse of the destiny God has for them seldom turn it down. The more common mistake is trying to activate it too soon in ways that may not be God. The common failure scenario is to idolize the pulpit ministry in their local church or the traveling ministry at the conference or on TV. If you happen to have a kingly calling (most of us do),

God isn't calling you to run away from your vocation. He knew all about your vocation before you got saved. He's planting people throughout our cities in business, education, the arts, and government so that all the bases are covered and He touches every corner with His Spirit.

> *Each one should remain in the situation which he was in when God called him. Were you a slave when you were called? Don't let it trouble you—although if you can gain your freedom, do so. For he who was a slave when he was called by the Lord is the Lord's freedman; similarly, he who was a free man when he was called is Christ's slave. You were bought at a price; do not become slaves of men. Brothers, each man, as responsible to God, should remain in the situation God called him to.* (I Cor. 7:20-24)

Chapter 22
His Relationships

Healthy relationships start from a true understanding of the nature of God and the nature of humanity. We worship the God of the Bible Who has made people with a free will. He wants us to cooperate with Him, but not merely through coercion. Our God is looking for relational people who share His heart and choose to co-labor with Him. This kind of relationship depends on God's willingness to talk with us and show us His plans—which He readily does.

Relating to the Father

Notice the relationship Jesus had with the Father.

> *Jesus gave them this answer: "I tell you the truth, the Son can do nothing by himself; he can do only what he sees his Father doing, because whatever the Father does the Son also does. For the Father loves the Son and shows him all he does...."* (John 5:19-20)

This is the type of relationship which you and I should have with the Father:

- We can do anything, but our power comes from doing what the Father does (vs. 19).
- The Father loves His children and shows them "everything" (vs. 20).
- We have authority and power to use at our discretion on the Father's behalf (vs. 21).

Relating to People

Given the correct image of God and the subsequent relationship with Him, how does this affect a King's relationships with others? To understand this, we need to know two facts about people:

1. People ultimately do what they want to do (not what anyone else wants).
2. We are each responsible for our own motivations.

Most relational problems occur when other people don't live up to our expectations. When this inevitably happens, we have two choices. We can exercise the authority model and try to command a change. Or we can try to relate to them. In the endeavor to relate, we may be able to see what's motivating them to act the way they do. If we understand their positions, we might have a chance to adjust their self-motivation. Or, we might need to adjust ours. At least we'll understand why they are behaving as they are.

Kings, Priests, Prophets, and parents—all people who carry authority—run into these situations all the time. Their response to people as leaders is directly related to the way they relate to God. If their God is an impersonal, unchangeable Force, Who demands submission, then the individual will tend to deal with others in an authoritarian way.

Here's an example from my own marriage. If Sue and I have a marital disagreement, I could sit her down and explain that the covenant of marriage is contractual in nature and that I'm the head of the house, according to Ephesians 5, and that she should obey me. She might respond—for a while—but sooner or later she will throw off that yoke of oppression. Somewhere between days and decades she will explode and the relationship will erode.

My second choice is to establish a relational connection with her. To do this, I need to recognize that God created her with a free will and that she's ultimately going to follow it, regardless of what I say. Indeed, she should act as a free individual since God created her in His image. In relating to her, my goals are for both of us to recognize the Lord's leading and for us to cooperate together with Him. This process is the simple essence of becoming one in marriage.

> *Husbands, in the same way be considerate as you live with your wives, and treat them with respect as the weaker partner and as heirs with you of the gracious gift of life, so that nothing will hinder your prayers.* (I Peter 3:7)

God is asking me to live with Sue in an understanding way so that He can answer my prayers. One of my goals in relating to Sue is to hear what God is putting into her heart. What's her dream? What is she feeling? Another goal is just to enjoy being with her as we ask and receive from the Father. Sue and I are heirs together of all that God has for us.

These same principles also apply to unifying a work force or bringing a church together. Kings must respect the free wills of others. The glue that holds us together is our ability to relate around the Father Himself and around the business in which He's inviting us to participate.

Leading a group of people with true relationships rather than just authoritative cooercion takes more work, time, and patience. Yet, the power released when people operate out of their own free wills is multiplied incredibly.

Relationships With the Unwilling

Marriage, work, church, and even living with ourselves, frequently puts us in the dilemma of being committed to live and work with people who don't always agree with us. What then?

First, we need to realize that God is in that situation with us fairly frequently. He's very gracious about showing us His will and waiting for us to warm to the idea He is presenting.

How do we make our vision contagious so that others want to participate out of their own free wills? How do we win them over?

I have noticed that effective Kings put others first

in their relationships. When they lead a conversation with me, eventually I begin unwittingly talking about myself. They care about connecting first and promoting their agenda second. They make friends rather than slaves.

This feels very different from talking to people who operate out of the authority and submission model. The authority types just want to talk about the plan instead of connecting with the people. They communicate a clear message that their plan is more important than their people who carry out the plan.

The Incentive Plan – An Open Heaven

The hidden truth in placing relationships first is that when everyone—leaders and workers, husbands and wives—get on the same page with regard to the Father's will, prayers get answered more readily, anointings flow freer, power (both spiritual and natural) becomes more abundant. When two or more of us see the same revelation of the Father's business and start to pray, the heavens open.

> *"I tell you the truth, whatever you bind on earth will be bound in heaven, and whatever you loose on earth will be loosed in heaven. Again, I tell you that if two of you on earth agree about anything you ask for, it will be done for you by my Father in heaven. For where two or three come together in my name, there am I with them."* (Matt. 18:18-20)

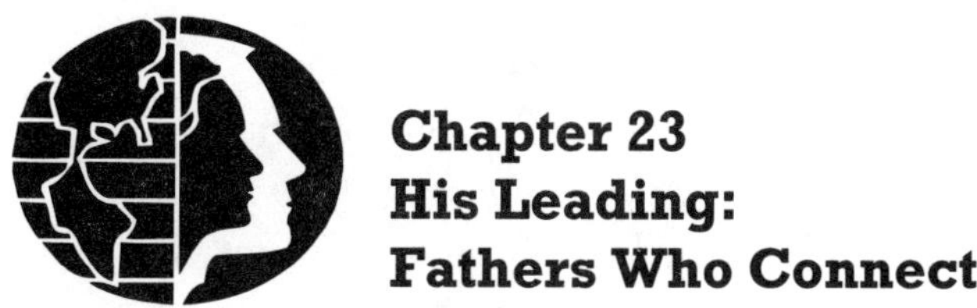

Chapter 23
His Leading:
Fathers Who Connect

Leaders in the church, as well as in business, politics, and even the home, often operate out of a control/authority model. They follow this pattern:

1. See a problem;
2. Figure out how to fix it;
3. Tell the people what do;
4. Expect the problem to be fixed.

This version of leadership is fatally flawed for many reasons. Primarily, it kills people's motivations because it ignores one simple fact of human nature: in the final analysis, people do what they want to do, not what they're told to do. Leaders who operate from the "God-is-a-force mentality" tend to lead from the authority/control model. In the process, they suck the life out of their followers by trying to make them work against their natures. These autocrats pick a path, issue orders, expect results, and when they find disobedience—whether in business or in the home—they fire their employees or spank their children or rebuke their spouses. We must stop pretending that people can be treated as commodities. It doesn't work.

Rather than imposing His will, God likes to work within our hearts, changing our desires to match His.

> *I will give you a new heart and put a new spirit in you; I will remove from you your heart of stone and give you a heart of flesh. And I will put my Spirit in you and move you to follow my decrees and be careful to keep my laws.* (Ez. 36:26-27)

There may be times when leaders must demand action from their people, but for the vast majority of the time effective leaders help people motivate themselves.

Many Church leaders I know suffer from a common malady summed up by the tired lament: "Nobody is following." Most business institutions have enough negative incentives to make people generally do what they have to do, whether or not they want to. They either work and marginally prosper, or get fired and starve. However, that isn't true in the Church. The threat of fire and brimstone doesn't scare people these days, so godly leaders have to lead in the way that God leads. Here are a few suggestions based on the biblical leadership model for all leaders.

1. Read minds with hearing hearts – Knowledge of what to do isn't really the first thing a leader must have. Most followers already know what needs to be done! Leadership starts by understanding what's in the followers' minds and hearts.

As a parent, the most significant thing I've ever done was listening to my kids and learning where their hearts were. Until I know their hearts, my leadership tends to be too dictatorial and they resist. If I can hear a follower's heart and know how they perceive me, then I can help them find a motive to follow the Lord. Just telling them what to do bypasses their God-given responsibility to be self-motivated, and it ignores my true responsibility as a leader to know my people.

2. Be bold in pursuing hearts – Kingly fathers, mothers, leaders, and husbands must have the courage to explore the hearts of others and help them find a motivation to obey God. It's a lot easier in the short-term just to tell people what to do, without connecting with their hearts and getting your hands dirty...but eventually it just builds a wall. We serve a generation that has been burned by autocrats who stayed on a pedestal and never knew their people. A connecting church starts with leaders who can connect. Kings will not expand God's Kingdom in the marketplace until they can relate.

3. Let emotions flow – People are emotional and they are powerfully motivated by their emotions. Connecting with people means connecting on an emotional level, which may feel messy for those of us not comfortable with our own emotions. As leaders, we are often more comfortable with a sterile environment. Connecting with people's feelings can be more like changing a diaper than designing a computer chip, but one is a necessity for the other. Get your hands dirty! I'm an engineer who was raised on a ranch in Montana. I'm not comfortable slobbering my emotions all over the counseling room floor. But I've had to learn that even God experiences emotions. Hence, we can know that it is part of our God-given nature to have emotions.

4. Respect people – Leaders often become leaders because they think they know what needs to be done, and they are ready to tell people what to do. When expectations are not met, however, it's also common for leaders of any type (managers, husbands, fathers, pastors, etc.) to get mad at their people for not following their directions. This is another problem with the authority/control leadership style.

Here's what I've learned in my own life as a pastor. People will respond to God's plan when the time is right. If people aren't following my plan, I need to look for a flaw in my leadership first, before accusing them of rebellion. The timing and the approach of my plan may need to be tweaked, or maybe I'm just plain wrong—a far more common occurrence than my people failing to respond. I don't follow the whims of the flock, but I do try to hear the voice of the Shepherd. The truth is that all of God's people can hear the voice of the Shepherd about as well as I can. Even in our national government, democracy works because the public is a lot smarter than some leaders would like to think. God respects people and so should we.

5. How to ask questions — Doctors often begin their diagnosis by asking, "What hurts?" The answer guides their next step. While the key to leadership is knowing people and connecting with God's leadership, this process starts by asking questions. When we ask people questions and allow them to question us, we acknowledge that they have a free will. This is the same way God deals with us.

> *"Come let us reason together, says the Lord. Though your sins be as scarlet, I shall make them white as snow."*
> (Is. 1:18) [Emp. Added]

Jesus taught His disciples largely by asking and answering questions. The real goal of godly leadership is to connect people with three simple things:

- **Your *kairos* moment (*kairos* is the Greek term for "present")**. What is God doing through the present circumstances in your life? It could be anything from blessing to discipline, promotion to character development. Seeing God in our present circumstances is a huge step toward relating to people in a way that helps them relate to God.

- **Your destiny**. What is the gifting in your life for the kind of ministry and motivation that you have? If we can connect people with their larger purposes in life, then all the preparations start to make sense.

- **Your obedience.** Most people do want to please God. When we can help them connect with a credible plan that includes their ability to hear God, they will respond to God. Everyone is wired with a deep hunger to relate to the Father and please Him. We're created with it. Motivation has roots in the individual calling that God gave us. Leaders really can't motivate people just by telling them what to do. Leaders can connect them with their destinies and their own God-inspired motivations.

Chapter 24
His Mentors and Mentoring

It would be interesting to go around to all the expensive houses in town and listen to the owners' life stories. I'd wager that most would have a story about how they were mentored by a parent, an uncle, or close advisor who instilled values and taught them the right way to do things. In many cases, I would expect to hear of a family business that had been passed down. These are not just idle musings on my part, but a pattern I have seen in successful lives from my years of working with people as a pastor, counselor, and businessman.

In our family, my mother taught my sister all about sewing at a young age; my dad had me on a horse at the age of six, doing a full day's work. I remember the cattle drives, branding calves, and trading work with the neighboring ranchers. My grandfather raised horses on the same land that our ranch is on today. Dad made his living raising cattle. He used horses on the ranch and made sure we had good ones to ride. He also made sure that we knew how to handle them. He had a teacher's ability to show me how to ride and train horses. When I was ten, he had raised a couple of colts, one of which he gave to me to break and call my own. She was a bay filly named Barbie. He never rode that horse, not once. Instead, he left her all to me. He showed me how to train her, step by step, from halter breaking to lead, to ground driving, to loping figure eight's, and finally, following a cow. His pride in my own progress with horses radiated through his tough exterior, but the progress of the colt was the loudest praise he ever could give me. She was a grand champion in 4H and she drew the compliments of the other ranchers with whom we rode.

Later, in my teens, there were other mentors: teachers, coaches, a doctor who led me to the Lord. They all had a blessed impact on me. But nothing has had a greater personal impact on my life or my confidence than the mentoring of my own father and the shaping environment of his peers in rural Montana.

Sure, we haven't all grown up on ranches. Some of us came of age in the inner city, others in the suburbs, while others had no fathers at all. Still, the principles are universal. Those of us who have become successful have had a mentor at some time in our lives. None of us are islands. We stand on the shoulders of those who equipped us for life.

Kings who are successful in their endeavors are the first to point to their mentors. They fondly speak of that molding process and the respect and love they have for the people who first took them by their hands to train them. Kings understand the importance of mentoring from their own experiences. They tend to be generous and willing to share their experiences with the next generation that follows.

Kings maintain mentoring relationships throughout their lives. Businesspeople help one another. Musicians teach one another and compare notes on opportunities and ideas. Politicians look out for one another. Kings are always participants in some kind of fraternity of relationships that helps their creative processes and improves the quality of their crafts. They enjoy helping their peers increase their successes. So successful is this type of mentoring that some people not familiar with it would consider it "cheating."

The stereotype of successful people is that they are aloof and loners. But that is an image created from not being a part of their inner circles. Successful people are made of the same stuff as the rest of us. They just have had a different mentoring process and a continuing circle of peers who facilitate their network. You can be equally successful in your sphere of influnece with skills, gifts, and destiny.

Think about making your dream a reality and begin to pray for it as though it were part of the inheritance God has for you. When you start down that road, God will lead you to someone who has done it before and has a heart to help you. Servants have task masters requiring them to do what they don't enjoy. Kings have mentors in the beginning and fraternities throughout life who share the secrets of their successes. If you could walk a mile in the shoes of someone after whom you want to model your life, you would find that their "miraculous" achievements were learned step by step, and that it's not as hard as you thought. In fact, if you had the same network of help, you could do the same things. When you see someone with a calling, gifting, and anointing similar to your own, you naturally will gravitate toward them. You'll experience a healthy envy that draws you into their anointing. They are examples which the Lord is showing you to pull you into your own destiny. Let your envy work its way into mentoring.

Jesus has gone before you. He's not only the King of kings, He's also the Mentor of mentors. He's bringing many sons to glory and He's not ashamed to call them brothers. He's gone before us and already has entered the place of our inheritance on our behalf.

> *In bringing many sons to glory, it was fitting that God, for whom and through whom everything exists, should make the author of their salvation perfect through suffering. Both the one who makes men holy and those who are made holy are of the same family. So Jesus is not ashamed to call them brothers.*
>
> (Heb. 2:10-11)

Jesus continues performing His mentoring ministry, both directly and through people. The mentoring process is the practical side of entering your inheritance.

We also need to realize that the next generation is intended by God to receive a double portion of everything we have. Think about it—more anointing and more financial promise. Historically, each generation since Adam and Eve progressively has been in a better position to experience God's blessings and to expand His Kingdom. Each succeeding generation stands on the shoulders of their forefathers and does even better. The "good old days" weren't all that good by any measure! In the next chapter we'll look at passing the baton to this "doubly anointed" generation.

> *When they had crossed, Elijah said to Elisha, "Tell me, what can I do for you before I am taken from you?" "Let me inherit a double portion of your spirit," Elisha replied. "You have asked a difficult thing," Elijah said, "yet if you see me when I am taken from you, it will be yours—otherwise not."*
>
> (II Kings 2:9-10)

Integrity—Part of Something Bigger

Mentors are not just advantageous, but essential. The biggest mistake Kings make is getting a glimpse of their ministry and trying to enter it too quickly. In this hour Kings are often coming out of an environment of rejection that left them without an appetite for being accountable. They simply have never experienced ministry or guidance from a mentor that leads to their success. They've felt the disqualification that goes with correction, but they've never known a leader that opened doors for them.

Face it, we all need help. Kings who are successful always have a network of advisors. Many delegate a means of veto to another as part of their accountability. Why? There is safety in a multitude of counselors (Proverbs 11:14, 24:6)

One of the definitions of integrity is to be part of something bigger. When we're alone we're broken. God uses the term "body" to describe how closely Christians should function together. Many think of guidance as something they get from God alone. In reality God speaks through people to provide a significant portion of our guidance.

> *The integrity of the upright shall guide them....*
> [Prov. 11:3 KJV]

The wealth, influence, and responsibility that will follow the ministry of Kings is great. We shouldn't be naive about the devices of the enemy or our own frailty. Mentoring and pastoring Kings with huge destinies will be on the critical path for this movement. Most of us can point to some personal shipwreck that could have been avoided if we'd been networked with the right mentor.

One of my personal dreams is to create a network of contacts that can provide the specialized help that Kings will need to start businesses, make investments, and launch ministries.

Chapter 25
His Legacy:
Passing the Baton

Much of our focus has been on possessing our inheritance. Now let's discuss passing it on. Our Western culture doesn't have the same emphasis on developing and passing on the family business from generation to generation as many other cultures have. Where they pass wealth from generation to generation, ours doesn't. Here are three reasons.

1. We value independence, exalt self-made people, and have little respect for those who have inherited wealth.
2. The Christian community generally has held an eschatology that teaches that the end of the world is at hand. Hence, we don't conceive of a future beyond the present generation, and we certainly don't have time to build wealth over several generations.
3. We have a transient lifestyle which also contributes to this phenomenon. We raise our kids, send them off to college, they get jobs in another state, and we hear from them once a year when a new grandchild is born. That is hardly a lifestyle in which to foster family business propagation.

I recently attended a class on shaping your career. The current emphasis in the ever-changing, fast-paced business community is being willing to change and move to new opportunities when old ones dry up. The instructor lived what he preached. He had been in a computer programming job for the first 15 years of his career and jumped at some of the high dollar opportunities that came with the dot-com boom. He made good money; changed jobs often, broadened his skills, and developed an outstanding resume. He was willing to move anywhere opportunities presented themselves. His wife and six kids were not in a position to go with him, so they lived apart for an extended period. He finally got a divorce and traveled from job to job with no permanent residence. He likely will make good money for the rest of his life, but he probably won't have much to pass on to his children. His broken family won't leave much opportunity to mentor his children, and his profession is too unstable to pass on as an inheritance.

This example illustrates the complexity of our lives in our hectic, changing society. Now, let's examine the blueprint for how our lives should appear.

Family Destiny

General counseling for people who are struggling with their lives usually includes teaching them a concept of inheriting the sinful traits of parents and ancestors and severing those generational ties with prayer. This teaching is based on a number of Scriptures, one of which is in Deuteronomy.

> *"...for I, the LORD your God, am a jealous God, punishing the children for the sin of the fathers to the third and fourth generation of those who hate me, but showing love to a thousand generations of those who love me and keep my commandments."* (Deut. 5:9-10)

Notice that God deals with sin to the third and fourth generation, but shows love to a thousand generations. This means that it's not just evil that gets passed down through generational lines. God's love and blessings get passed down, as well, and they overtake the evil after the fourth generation.

When we think of our calling or destiny, we typically think of our own lives. However, our ministry gifts and calling also have a generational aspect. We inherit part of our destiny from the calling God has on our parents, and the thread from them goes back a thousand generations. It's also our responsibility to pass that inherited calling down to our children and grandchildren. The Bible speaks of a natural inheritance and a spiritual inheritance. It is our responsibility to train our children to receive both.

My Personal Testimony

As a pastor and an engineer, when I thought about the idea of generational destiny, a couple of things provided clues as to what God had in mind for me. Both my father and grandfather raised horses and cattle. They were ranchers, although today it is called animal husbandry. As a pastor, I shepherd people.

My dad's ability to teach me how to train horses and a multitude of other ranch jobs was a premonition of the teaching gift that I have in my own life. When he was in high school, he was tall and perhaps a little somber. Although he now goes to church and is saved, he was never big on spiritual things when I was a child. One day we found his high school annual from 1931. Friends wrote notes in the margins. My dad's nickname in high school was "Reverend Garfield," apparently because he looked mature for his age and took life too seriously. As His son, I'm now a literal "reverend."

My grandfather was the first elected sheriff in our county in Montana. My grandmother finished his term after he was killed in the line of duty and she was elected for another term after that. My grandfather on my mother's side was a mine superintendent. That's probably where my leadership and managerial skills originated.

If you look at your own inheritance, there will be a theme and connections hinting at the plan of God that spans multiple generations. When he was five, our son Ben went with us to an outdoor Christian rock concert filled with 25,000 people. He was so enthralled with the whole event that he looked up and told me that he wanted to be a pastor when he grew up. Regardless of what he finally does with his life, this statement reflected a generational tug on his heart to follow God's destiny for our family.

Passing the Baton

There is a destiny on your life. It's a package of blessings, abilities, gifts, and fruit that are both spiritual and financial. You have a responsibility to pass that package on to your children. To do this, develop a plan to train them to receive it. You also may have to help them deal with the fact that they will inherit some of your destiny and become similar to you, even though they might not wish to do so. Assume that the promises that go with your destiny are big enough to require several generations to possess them.

> *A good man leaves an inheritance for his children's children, but a sinner's wealth is stored up for the righteous.*
> (Prov. 13:22)

> *Houses and wealth are inherited from parents, but a prudent wife is from the LORD.* (Prov. 19:14)

> *Who, then, is the man that fears the LORD? He will instruct him in the way chosen for him. He will spend his days in prosperity, and his descendants will inherit the land.* (Ps. 25:12-13)

> *...children should not have to save up for their parents, but parents for their children.* (II Cor. 12:14)

Conclusion: Where Do We Go from Here?

People take great delight in being used by God for His purposes. At some level, however, people called to be Kings have felt left behind and rejected over the frustration of not finding an expression for their ministries in their local churches. In reality, the great task of the Church is to "equip the saints for the work of the ministry." The real work of the ministry is in the marketplace. It is the saints who will do it—we call them Kings.

Taking Action

When I preached this message in our church, it caused us to dream and act. We caught a vision for our personal inheritance in God and began to contend for it in prayer. It fueled a healthy motivation to identify and embrace the practical side of our personal destinies.

- Two people started businesses that made room for ministry. Evangelism and prayer counseling occurred right in the workplace.
- One person went back to school to start the vocation of which he always had dreamed.
- One person started a healing ministry.
- Other people took interest in investments and real estate to raise funds for missions and ministry.

Why did this happen? We each felt the Lord personally inviting us to a deeper expression of His destiny for us. It was exciting! Releasing Kings for marketplace ministry strikes a responsive cord in the hearts of people.

Now Prophesy It!

Lord, we declare freedom—for your people to pursue the desires You've placed within them. We embrace the desires You've placed within our own hearts. We claim Your protection over our frailties, and we're grateful for Jesus' advocacy in intercession on our behalf.

Thank You, for creating us in Your image with an ability to fulfill all of Your will. We confess our desire to see Your purposes on Earth established. We seek Your Kingdom first and long to be filled with Your Spirit. We admit to ourselves that we're not consumed with sin but, because of You, we are free from the power of wrong desires and bad habits. We release our hearts from the fear of pursuing dreams—the fear of attempting the goodness and greatness of Your plans in our hearts. We step forth in faith!

As a river flowing from Your Temple, we command a release of boldness. We release dreams and visions for great things in the hearts of all Your people. We command the release of Kings to flow out of Your Church and bless the marketplaces of our cities with passion and creativity. We command an anointing of confidence and prosperity upon Your people that only can be attributed to the movement of Your Spirit. We release a people who are seated at Your right hand, who no longer are content to live in the valleys, but have hearts to live with You on the mountaintops.

We proclaim an era of abundance on Your people that flows through their marriages and families, their businesses, their finances, and their occupations. We declare rivers of living water to flow from Your people to bless our cities, our nation, and the nations of this world. We bless the marketplace with the ministry of Kings. Let Your name be glorified in the arts, in education, in governments, and in businesses throughout this land. Let us pick up the mantle for revival and bring it to our nation. Let the visions and dreams and the resources multiply among Your people in a contagious move of Your Spirit that sweeps over our land. Let Kings arise and enthrone the King of kings.

It Is Time Now!

- Businesspeople: do commerce, increase sales, make a profit;
- Teachers: train, speak, mold character;
- Politicians: influence, stand up, demand change;
- Entertainers: make us laugh, make us cry, make us think;
- Artists: form our values, stir emotions, seize our thoughts;

- Craftsmen: build, design, and serve humanity, giving God the glory;
- Stars, heroes, personalities, and all those in the spotlight: be worthy of our adulation;
- Entrepreneurs: invent, build, and create;
- Engineers: fill the Earth and subdue it; create abundance for everyone;
- Parents: love and be there for the next generation;
- Government leaders: establish peace and order, care for the needy, and rule in righteousness.

Marketplace Ministry provides a revolutionary format to fulfill the Great Commission. It facilitates a synergy between Kings and Priests. It enables God's children to take their inheritance.

> *"Ask of me, and I will make the nations your inheritance, the ends of the earth your possession."* (Ps. 2:8)

Appendix A

Further Your Passion for the Kingdom

This book can't be read without dreaming about unlimited possibilities. The Lord will speak to you about the desires of your heart once you give yourself permission to go there. He also will speak to you about the how's and when's.

As He does, we would like to help you network with other people, organizations, and resources through a website. The Lord is moving so quickly that the Internet is the only viable means of keeping pace with all that's unfolding. The Web Site is:

http://www.releasing-kings.com

Your next step may be much more practical than you realize, and our hope is to use this website as a springboard to new ideas for ministry in the marketplace and new ideas for helping Kings tap into the "power to get wealth" (Deut. 8:18). Both the spirit of the message and the passion of the people are highly contagious. Get closer and you will catch it!

Appendix B

Spread the Good News

You can obtain additional copies of *Releasing Kings in the Marketplace,* through either of the following websites:

http://www.releasing-kings.com

http://www.worldcastministries.com

Discounts are available for bookstores and quantity orders.

Appendix C

The Network to Release Young Kings

One of the most exciting outgrowths of the current emphasis on Marketplace Ministry is the work of *Threshold Resourcing, Inc.,* which creates a way for successful Christian businesspeople to mentor young entrepreneurs. My own son participated in a pilot program that changed both his life and mine. At 18 years old he had the opportunity to learn everything from starting a checking account, to selling on E-bay, to opening a Limited Liability Company, to real estate investments, to financial planning for retirement. He has learned the things I wish I had known at his age. The year-long program was done within the local church and under the oversight of experienced business and community leaders. It has provided him with a network of professional relationships that will help him for the rest of his life.

I wish tens of thousands of Christian leaders would take advantage of the ministry of *Threshold Resourcing, Inc.* and follow through to establish "entrepreneurial clubs" in their churches or Christian communities. It gives the businesspeople in their churches a place of honor and recognition in their roles in expanding the Kingdom of God. It moves businesspeople into positions of mentoring the younger generation. It will have a far-reaching impact upon our communities as these young people emerge in their ministries and vocations. And it will produce wealth for the local church and the worldwide expansion of the Kingdom of God.

For more information concerning *Threshold Resourcing, Inc.*, *Threshold Resources,* or *"The Network,"* please see:

www.thenetwrk.com

Appendix D
Other Books by Harold R. Eberle
which further develop the theology behind Marketplace Ministry

BRINGING THE FUTURE INTO FOCUS

An Introduction to the Progressive Christian Worldview

What does the future hold? Will there be peace or war? Are the people of God going to rise up in glory and unity or will they be overcome by apathy and deception? Is Jesus coming for a spotless Bride or is He going to rescue a tattered band of zealots out of a wicked chaotic mess? Where is God taking humanity in the Twenty-First Century?

This book will answer your questions and fill you with hope.

WHO IS GOD?

WHAT IS HE DOING? WHO AM I? WHY IS THERE SUFFERING AND PAIN?

This is an in-depth teaching on the nature of God and humanity. This new book is radical, bold, and captivating, yet already has the endorsements of some of the most influential Christian leaders in the world. This book is soon to be released in hard copy, but presently you can download it from the web sight of Worldcast Publishing:

www.worldcastpublishing.com

PRECIOUS IN HIS SIGHT *A Fresh Look at the Nature of Man*

During the Fourth Century Augustine taught about the nature of man using as his key Scripture a verse in the book of Romans which had been mistranslated. Since that time the Church has embraced a false concept of humanity which has negatively influenced every area of Christianity. It is time for Christians to come out of darkness! This book, considered by many to be Harold Eberle's greatest work, has implications upon our understanding of sin, salvation, Who God is, evangelism, the world around us and how we can live the daily, victorious lifestyle.

DEVELOPING A PROSPEROUS SOUL

VOL I: **HOW TO OVERCOME A POVERTY MIND-SET**

VOL II: **HOW TO MOVE INTO**

GOD'S FINANCIAL BLESSINGS

There are fundamental changes you can make in the way you think which will help release God's blessings. This is a balanced look at the promises of God with practical steps you can take to move into financial freedom. It is time for Christians to recapture the financial arena.

Other Books by Harold R. Eberle

THE COMPLETE WINESKIN (Fourth edition)

The Body of Christ is in a reformation. God is pouring out the Holy Spirit and our wineskins must be changed to handle the new wine. Will the Church come together in unity? Where do small group meetings fit? How does the anointing of God work and what is your role? What is the 5-fold ministry? How are apostles, prophets, evangelists, pastors and teachers going to rise up and work together? This book puts into words what you have been sensing in your spirit. (Eberle's best seller, translated into many languages, distributed worldwide.)

GRACE...THE POWER TO REIGN

The Light Shining from Romans 5-8

We struggle against sin and yearn for God's highest. Yet, on a bad day it is as as if we are fighting with gravity. Questions go unanswered:

- Where is the power to overcome temptations and trials?
- Is God really willing to breathe into us so that these dry bones can live and we may stand strong?

For anyone who ever has clenched his fist in the struggle to live godly, here are the answers.

GOD'S LEADERS FOR TOMORROW'S WORLD

(Revised/expanded edition) You sense a call to leadership in your life, but questions persist: "Does God want me to rise up? Is this pride? Do I truly know where to lead? How can I influence people?" Through a new understanding of leadership dynamics, learn how to develop godly charisma. Confusion will melt into order when you see the God-ordained lines of authority. Fear of leadership will change to confidence as you learn to handle power struggles. Move into your "metron," that is, your God-given authority. You can be all God created you to be!

SPIRITUAL REALITIES

Here they are—Harold Eberle's six volumes explaining how the spiritual and natural worlds relate and interact.

Other Books by Harold R. Eberle

If God is Good, Why is there so much Suffering and Pain?

Life isn't fair! Terrorist bombings. Ethnic cleansing. Body-ravaging diseases. Murder. Child abuse. Natural disasters. Genetic maladies. These travesties, global and seemingly relentless, drive us to the limits of our reasoning. When pain and suffering invade our well-laid plans for a good life, we ask the gut question: Why, God, why? In this book, Harold R. Eberle evaluates the role God plays in the Earth, explores the origin of suffering, and reassures us of God kind intentions toward us.

Two Become One (Second edition)

Releasing God's Power for Romance, Sexual Freedom and Blessings in Marriage

Kindle afresh the "buzz of love." Find out how to make God's law of binding forces work for you instead of against you. The keys to a thrilling, passionate, and fulfilling marriage can be yours if you want them. This book is of great benefit to pastors, counselors, young singles, divorcees and especially married people. Couples are encouraged to read it together.

You Shall Receive Power

God's Spirit will fill you in measures beyond what you are experiencing presently. This is not just about Pentecostal or Charismatic blessings. There is something greater. It is for all Christians, and it will build a bridge between those Christians who speak in tongues and those who do not. It is time for the whole Church to take a fresh look at the work of the Holy Spirit in our individual lives. This book will help you. It will challenge you, broaden your perspective, set you rejoicing, fill you with hope, and leave you longing for more of God.

To place an order or to check current prices call:
1-800-308-5837 within the USA or:
509-248-5837 from outside the USA

Worldcast Publishing
P.O. Box 10653
Yakima, WA 98909-1653

E-mail: office@worldcastpublishing.com
Web Site: www.worldcastpublishing.com